# REFRAMING

[40 DAYS TO REFRAME & REFRESH YOUR LIFE]

ALISA HOPE WAGNER

MARKED WRITERS PUBLISHING

REFRAMING: 40 DAYS TO REFRAME & REFRESH YOUR LIFE

Marked Writers Publishing
www.alisahopewagner.com

Scriptures taken from various translations of the Bible found at www.biblegateway.com

Cover design by Alisa Hope Wagner
Author Photo by Monica Lugo

ISBN-13: 9798985066272

# REFRAMING

[40 DAYS TO REFRAME & REFRESH YOUR LIFE]

# DEDICATION

Daniel – the man of my dreams

Isaac Jeremiah – my prophet

Levi Daniel – my shepherd

Karis Ruth – my graceful companion

Editing Team – Patricia Coughlin, Shay Lee & Faith Newton

Holy Spirit – my writing partner

# HANGING HAMMOCKS OF REST

*Reframe:*

*verb*

- To frame or express (words or a concept or plan) differently.

I have learned much of the negativity in my life is due to my own faulty perceptions. God's Word has the Truth and reading and meditating on it will truly set us free from the worries and the cares of this world. In fact, when we reframe everything (people and situations) within the guidance of the Bible, our minds can be both transformed and renewed (Romans 12.2). And once our minds (thoughts and imaginings) are renewed, our hearts (emotions and feelings) and our will (actions and behaviors) will follow suit.

Reframing takes practice at first because we are capturing every thought and working to transform what appears to be negative by sight into the parameters of God's Truth by faith (2 Corinthians 5.7). However, let me suggest we imagine the process like stringing up hammocks throughout our day. Sure, hanging a hammock can be a little awkward, but once it's up, we can lay back and rest in its embrace. When we are faced with something that aims to discourage us, we can restring our thoughts in expectation of God's goodness and provision.

As we renew our minds each day, we will ensure that negative thoughts do not gather and collect, creating a heavy quilt of discouragement, depression and bitterness over us. This heaviness will prevent us from living God's best life for us, and it will weigh us down, making it difficult to stand firm on God's promises. It's time to stop allowing negative thoughts to bully us. We must do as the Bible says and "...take captive every thought to make it obedient to Christ" (2 Corinthians 10.5 NIV).

In this 40-day devotional book, I offer simple, biblical ways you can hang hammocks and achieve God's rest every day. Remember, Jesus did the heavy lifting by dying on the cross to save us from our sins and reconcile us back to God. All we have to do is rest in the Finished Work of Jesus on the Cross. Every moment of the day, Jesus has a hammock ready for us to string up. We simply need to reframe our thoughts and rest in Him.

> "Come to me, all you who are weary and burdened, and I will give you rest. Take my yoke upon you and learn from me, for I am gentle and humble in heart, and you will find rest for your souls. For my yoke is easy and my burden is light" (Matthew 11.28-30 NIV).

# TABLE OF CONTENTS

# DAY 1

## [8 BIBLE VERSES TO OVERCOME FEAR]

My middle child, who was 11 years old at the time, began to have a serious fear of choking. The fear was irrational and probably stemmed from me. I have enlarged tonsils, which caused me to have frequent sore throats when I was young and difficulty swallowing. I still sometimes choke as an adult if I don't chew my food thoroughly. I'm used to it now, so I tend not to notice. I assume my son saw a few of my choking fits and fear lodged itself deep within him.

My son's fear moved beyond a simple explanation, however, and into a spiritual battle. The enemy took that fear and ran with it. Just like a lion, the enemy looks to attack the weak, isolated and the young. My son is young, and the enemy does not play fair. He used that fear to oppress and torment my son every single day and night for weeks.

> "Stay alert! Watch out for your great enemy, the devil. He prowls around like a roaring lion, looking for someone to devour" (1 Peter 5.8 NLT).

**How Fear Becomes a Battle**.

My son's fear of choking became so consuming that he wouldn't eat, and he began to lose weight. He was tormented by the fear and cried out to me several times. I would pray over him, but it wasn't working. Finally, we were in the car one day, and he broke down again. I had experienced a similar battle with fear when I was his age, and I knew if I didn't uproot it now, it would stay tucked inside of him like shrapnel.

Finally, I had it. I knew right then and there; this fear wasn't caused by stress or a need for attention or a projection of worry. This fear was an attack of the enemy, and this mom was ready to fight! Although I am not strong enough, I know the One Who is. He is the Creator of the heavens and earth, and everything including fear bows to Him.

> "Everything on earth will worship you; they will sing your praises, shouting your name in glorious songs" (Psalm 66.4 NLT).

**How Fear Gets Demolished.**

I know that the name of Jesus is powerful. I know that the enemy must flee from His name. I know that there is power in the Blood of Jesus. And I know that FEAR BOWS TO THE CROSS!

I stepped into the supernatural realm, and I stood in God's throne room with my son at my side. I waged war against an enemy who wants nothing more than to torment my kid with fear. I told the enemy he had no authority here. I looked toward heaven and proclaimed that my son is co-heirs with Christ. He is God's beloved son. He walks in God's authority. And I banned the devil from messing with my son.

And it worked. That night I told my son that he might have residual feelings, like waking up from a nightmare, but the root fear had been banished. After that, my son began to eat more, and now six months later, my son has not mentioned anything about choking. What the enemy meant for evil; God turned to good. Now my son knows that he has the victory in Christ. He is stronger because he knows how to overcome fear.

> "You intended to harm me, but God intended it all for good. He brought me to this position so I could save the lives of many people" (Genesis 50.20 NLT).

**First, There is No Fear in Words of Life.**

> "Death and life are in the power of the tongue, And those who love it and indulge it will eat its fruit and bear the consequences of their words" (Proverbs 18.21 AMP).

I realize now that my kids are always watching and listening to me. I need to be careful about what I say in front of them. I don't want to say negative words of fear. Instead, I want to say overcoming words of faith. This doesn't mean that I'm untouched by the fact that we live in a fallen world. It does mean, however, that I am tapped into the limitless power of God through Jesus Christ. Whenever I feel the weight of fear on my own shoulders, I must automatically transform them into words of life.

**Second, There is No Fear in Jesus' Name.**

> "Therefore, God elevated him to the place of highest honor and gave him the name above all other names, that at the name of Jesus every knee should

bow, in heaven and on earth and under the earth" (Philippians 2.9-10 NLT).

Every knee bows to the name of Jesus. That name has so much power that it can vanquish all the enemies around us, including fear. I always tell my kids one thing: The name of Jesus is the most powerful thing in the universe. But they must not simply say the name, Jesus. They must be full of the belief that the name of Jesus is mighty. I demonstrate using the name of Jesus in my life. When I know that the enemy is trying to make my life difficult, I speak in the name of Jesus to overcome the devil's tactics!

**Third, There is No Fear in the Cross.**

> "He himself bore our sins in his body on the tree, that we might die to sin and live to righteousness. By his wounds you have been healed" (1 Peter 2.24 ESV).

The Cross is everything. The Cross is the key that unlocks power, life, joy, peace, healing and eternity. The Blood that dripped from the Cross caused a mighty outbreak of grace, mercy, and love to spread across space and time. We are healed from torment and oppression that are caused by fear. When we fully understand the resurrection power that occurred on the Cross, fear becomes so small, like a fly buzzing around our heads. All we need is to swat fear away.

**Fourth, There is no Fear in God's Authority.**

> "I have given you authority to trample on snakes and scorpions and to overcome all the power of the enemy; nothing will harm you" (Luke 10.19 NIV).

We have all authority through Jesus Christ. We have authority over our circumstances. We have authority over our enemy. And, yes, we have authority over our fears. Through Jesus Christ, we have the authority to trample over snakes and scorpions. These are symbols of demonic attacks that the enemy pushes our way. We can open our eyes to our authority in Christ, so we can then pass that authority to our kids.

**Fifth, There is No Fear in Peace.**

> "I am leaving you with a gift—peace of mind and heart. And the peace I give is a gift the world cannot give. So don't be troubled or afraid" (John 14.27 NLT).

Before Jesus left earth to go to the right hand of His Father, He left us His peace. This peace is like the eye of a hurricane. Regardless of the storm raging around us, we can have peace knowing that the Prince of Peace is living in our hearts. We simply need to be aware of this supernatural peace and walk in it. Fear has no room in a heart that is ruled by the Prince of Peace (Isaiah 9.6).

**Sixth, There is No Fear in the Father's House.**

> "So you have not received a spirit that makes you fearful slaves. Instead, you received God's Spirit when he adopted you as his own children. Now we call him, "Abba, Father" (Romans 8.15 NLT).

Through Jesus Christ, we are now called God's Children. Since God is our Father, and He is perfect, we have nothing to fear. As long as we stay tucked into His will, all the demonic forces can't torment or oppress us anymore. We simply need to imagine ourselves in the loving hands of God because fear can't reside there.

**Seventh, There is No Fear in Love.**

> "There is no fear in love. But perfect love drives out fear because fear has to do with punishment. The one who fears is not made perfect in love" (1 John 4.18 NIV).

Once we and our kids understand how fully and completely we are loved by God, we won't need to fear anymore. Valuable things are held onto protectively and tenderly. They are not handled with carelessness. God loves us, and we are precious in His sight. He is gentle and loving, and we don't have to fear. God is strong in us. He will fight the battle for us.

**Eighth, There is no Fear with God on our Side.**

> "Fear not, for I am with you; be not dismayed, for I am your God; I will strengthen you, I will help you, I will uphold you with my righteous right hand" (Isaiah 41.10 ESV).

God is always with us. We don't have to be afraid of anything. When we are weak, He is strong. God's righteous hand always holds us up. When we are afraid, we must know that God is bigger and stronger than our fear. Our proper understanding of how great and mighty God is will enable us to overcome all our fears. Fears fade quickly under the awesome presence of our God. If God is for us, who can be against us (Romans 8.31)?

# DAY 2

# [5 HABITS TO BRING JESUS INTO YOUR MORNING]

Ever since my kids were young, I have cultivated a morning routine that centers around Jesus every day. Yes, some days are more hectic than others. However, as a rule, we have 5 morning habits that prevent stress and start our day with Jesus. This morning routine is a simple way to show my kids how to walk in victory with Jesus.

My kids have been doing the same routine since they can remember. It has become a part of their lifestyle, which is exactly what I hoped for. I want these 5 habits to stick with them even when they leave the house. I want Jesus to be so a part of their day that it feels strange if they start their morning without Him.

**Why Starting the Day with Jesus is Important.**

First, I want my kids to know that they are not alone. My influence over their lives only goes so far. I am only human, and I can't be everything to them at every moment. But God is everywhere always. He is all-powerful and all-encompassing. I want my kids to have the habit of trusting God. When they can't rely on me, they can always rely on God.

> "The Lord your God is with you, the Mighty Warrior who saves. He will take great delight in you; in his

love he will no longer rebuke you, but will rejoice over you with singing" (Zephaniah 3.17 NIV).

Second, I want my kids to know that they are loved. Jesus loves my kids so much that He would die for them. I need my kids to know this truth. I can't expect them to love Jesus until they discover they are loved by Him. I want them to form a habit of carrying God's love for them wherever they go. Once they recognize and feel His love, they can reciprocate it.

> "For I am convinced that neither death nor life, neither angels nor demons, neither the present nor the future, nor any powers, neither height nor depth, nor anything else in all creation, will be able to separate us from the love of God that is in Christ Jesus our Lord" (Romans 8.38-39 NIV).

Third, I want my kids to have the power of Christ in their day. Our world is both physical and spiritual. I want my kids to not only have physical healthy habits but spiritual healthy habits also. They will need to develop a daily routine centered on Christ to live in His victory every day. The routine starts when they're young and will continue as they grow in their relationship with Christ.

> For everyone born of God is victorious and overcomes the world; and this is the victory that has conquered and overcome the world—our [continuing, persistent] faith [in Jesus the Son of God]" (1 John 5.4 AMP).

**Family Morning Habit #1: I Encourage Myself in the Lord.**

I can't expect my kids to start their day with Jesus if I don't. The first habit I do every morning is to encourage myself in the Lord. I remind myself that I am loved and blessed. Then I scrape away every fear, doubt, anxiety and worry. My kids are sponges and they will soak up whatever atmosphere I create for them. No matter our family circumstances and what is facing our day, I do as King David did and strengthen myself in the Lord.

> "...But David strengthened himself in the LORD his God" (1 Samuel 30.6 ESV).

**Family Morning Habit #2: Wake up on Time.**

I know this is simple but waking up on time will start the entire day with less stress. I make it a habit to wake my kids up an hour before we need to leave. This gives us plenty of time to ease into our day. Waking up on time is a habit that contributes to having a peaceful and joyful morning. Waking up early is a morning routine that will open the door to the other morning habits with Jesus.

> "Let me hear Your loving kindness in the morning, For I trust in You. Teach me the way in which I should walk, For I lift up my soul to You" (Psalm 143.8 AMP).

**Family Morning Habit #3: Motivating Words and Touch.**

I personally go to each of my kids' bedrooms and tell them something positive about the day to motivate them awake. I pet their heads and backs and tell them how handsome, beautiful, smart, talented and loved they all are. Also, I make a habit of giving them a little motivation for the day. I make it a routine to remind them of any special nugget that makes that day a gift. With God there is always something to look forward to!

> "Because of the Lord's great love we are not consumed, for his compassions never fail. They are new every morning; great is your faithfulness" (Lamentations 3.22-23 NIV).

**Family Morning Habit #4: Prayer during Breakfast.**

The morning prayer is not simply a prayer of grace for our food. I have a routine of praying for my individual kids and each one's day. I pray that God leads them and blesses them. I pray that they are protected from evil. I acknowledge that God will be with them throughout the day. I want them to have a habit of recognizing God's presence in their lives through prayer.

> *"Father, I pray for my son today. Let Him have the mind of Christ. Show Yourself to Him in a special way. Guide his steps at school. Protect Him from harm. Let Him know that You are always with Him. In Jesus' name amen."*

**Family Morning Habit #5: Daily Devotional or Scripture.**

We have read many family devotionals through the years. I started with simple devotionals for small children and toddlers. I have since moved up to devotionals for bigger kids. I even read the daily devotional I wrote, *Slay the Day*, to them. We make it a daily routine to read devotionals or several Scriptures from the Bible each morning. I read these words to them while they eat their breakfast. Therefore, they will not only be physically and spiritually fed, but equipped for the day.

> "All Scripture is God-breathed and is useful for teaching, rebuking, correcting and training in righteousness, so that the servant of God may be thoroughly equipped for every good work" (2 Timothy 3.16-17 NIV).

# DAY 3

## [7 TYPES OF FASTS AND 7 SPIRITUAL BENEFITS]

Toward the end of a five-day fast, I drove to a café to get my husband a latte. I was blown away by the intensity of my sense of smell. The ardent aroma of roasted coffee beans and the rich scent of frothed milk piqued my salivary glands. Fasting created a new physical and spiritual awareness to God's bounty in my life. When I finally was able to drink my own, I was in awe of God's goodness.

All throughout history, there were seasons of feast and famine. The body and soul naturally went through times of hard work and lack and times of ease and abundance. However, today in western culture, we have 365 days of abundance. Our diet is not dependent on the weather, season or location. We can eat all kinds of foods anytime we want, depending on our cravings.

With all this abundance of foods comes a greater need for self-control. We must decide the kinds and amounts of food that are appropriate for a healthy lifestyle. But even with a healthy standard of eating, we most likely won't experience famine without choosing it. Our bodies were designed to experience both feast and famine. We feast to celebrate. We fast to transform.

**The Physical Benefits of Fasting are Numerous.**

Although this article is about the spiritual benefits of fasting, I wanted to highlight 5 of the physical benefits since our flesh is so strongly entwined with our spirit.

- Fasting decreases food-related inflammation: Overconsumption of certain foods, like refined sugar, carbs, dairy and meat, can cause inflammation in the body. Fasting can decrease the inflammation created by too much of these foods.

- Fasting improves cell recycling: When we fast, our body has to recycle our own cells for energy. Our body consumes unhealthy cells first which can include pre-cancer and other dysfunctional cells.

- Fasting energizes your metabolism: Fasting for short periods of time can increase our metabolism since it must rev up to burn the body's fat storage.

- Fasting normalizes insulin sensitivity. Insulin resistance occurs when we consume too much sugar and carbs, which often leads to weight-related diseases. Fasting can reverse insulin resistance in the body.

- Fasting promotes weight loss: Fasting creates a caloric deficit, which aids in losing those extra pounds gathered from too much feasting.

**The Spiritual Benefits of Fasting are also Numerous.**

Since the spiritual world usurps the physical world, these benefits shape our life and the world around us. Before fasting, however, make sure that you have the grace to fast.

Sometimes when we feel like our life is falling apart, we try to fast. This to me is the worst time to fast because we are already under great amounts of stress. Fasting should only be done if the Holy Spirit is prompting us to fast. When it is God's will for us to fast, He will give us the grace to commit to it. However, it is always best to consult a doctor before fasting.

> "What is more pleasing to the Lord: your burnt offerings and sacrifices or your obedience to his voice? Listen! Obedience is better than sacrifice, and submission is better than offering the fat of rams" (1 Samuel 15.22 NLT).

**Spiritual Benefit #1: Fasting Causes us to Rely on God.**

Food is one of the basic needs of life. Physical hunger is not a pleasant experience. It can be a difficult trial to endure, but God's grace rises in our lives during hard times. When we fast, it forces us to seek God and lean into Him for help and comfort. God meets us powerfully during times we are desperate for Him. Fasting shows God that our hunger for Him surpasses our hunger for anything else.

> "You, God, are my God, earnestly I seek you; I thirst for you, my whole being longs for you, in a dry and parched land where there is no water" (Psalm 63.1 NIV).

> "But seek first his kingdom and his righteousness, and all these things will be given to you as well" (Matthew 6.33 NIV).

**Spiritual Benefit #2: Fasting Helps us be Filled with the Fruits of the Spirit.**

When we fast, we can become irritable and negative because our flesh is not happy. However, God calls us to allow Him to produce the Fruits of the Spirit within us. Fasting forces us to bypass the emotions of our flesh (which tend to be negative when hungry) and reach for divine emotions given to us through Jesus Christ. When we feel "hangry," we can grow our capacity under stress and choose to demonstrate goodness, gentleness and self-control.

> "But the fruit of the Spirit is love, joy, peace, forbearance, kindness, goodness, faithfulness, gentleness and self-control. Against such things there is no law" (Galatians 5.22-23 NIV).

**Spiritual Benefit #3: Fasting Opens our Heart to Hearing God's Voice.**

When we fast, we must focus on something else other than our hunger. This causes us to listen for God's voice since it is He who has called us to the fast. We have emptied ourselves of our most basic needs, so we can put our full attention on God. This is the best time to make those difficult choices in life. When we are at a crossroads and don't know which way to turn, fasting helps us to hear God's direction. As we walk in the Spirit, we won't be hung up by the desires of our flesh trying to hold us down and keep us off course. We will be able to hear more clearly from God when our spirit is stronger than our flesh.

"So I say, walk by the Spirit, and you will not gratify the desires of the flesh" (Galatians 5.16 NIV).

**Spiritual Benefit #4: Fasting Renews our Appreciation for God and His Blessings.**

We tend to forget how blessed we are. What once satisfied us now isn't enough. More food, more clothes, more entertainment, more trips. Whatever it is, we can forget how much God has given us, and our unquenchable desires become stronger than our love for God. When we take God's blessings for granted, we take Him for granted. But God wants our hearts to be turned toward Him. He wants us to appreciate all that He has done in our lives. When we fast, we force are hearts to turn to God, and we gain a renewed appreciation for God's presence in our lives. Our relationship with God is only possible through the Finished Work of Jesus Christ on the Cross. To know we will never be separated from God for all eternity is the ultimate blessing!

> "That is why the Lord says, 'Turn to me now, while there is time. Give me your hearts. Come with fasting, weeping, and mourning'" (Joel 2.12 NLT).

> "But God showed his great love for us by sending Christ to die for us while we were still sinners" (Romans 5.8 NLT).

**Spiritual Benefit #5: Fasting Gives Power to our Prayers.**

Jesus said there are some breakthroughs that are only gotten through prayer and fasting. If we have been facing the same unanswered prayer for a long time, it may be time to fast. Prayer that is powered by both faith and fasting can be the very force that unleashes God's promises in our lives. There are some evil spirits, like the spirit of lack and the hindering spirit, waging war against our promises, and we want to fast for added power to defeat them.

> "Afterward, when Jesus was alone in the house with his disciples, they asked him, 'Why couldn't we cast out that evil spirit?' Jesus replied, 'This kind can be cast out only by prayer'" (Mark 9.28-29 NLT).

**Spiritual Benefit #6: Fasting Creates an Environment for Miracles.**

Fasting forces the flesh to go under the authority of God's Spirit within us. When we are fasting, we are letting God have all the room. His Spirit becomes powerful and mighty in our words and actions. This is the perfect atmosphere for heaven to touch earth and transform our circumstances of lack, chaos and fear into God's ordained circumstances of supply, peace and faith. However, we must ensure that our fast is done for heavenly rewards, not earthly rewards. God blesses us when we keep our fast secret unless our testimony of fasting is used to edify others.

> "When you fast, do not look somber as the hypocrites do, for they disfigure their faces to show others they are fasting. Truly I tell you, they have received their reward in full. But when you fast, put oil on your head and wash your face, so that it will not be obvious to others that you are fasting, but only to your Father, who is unseen; and your Father, who sees what is done in secret, will reward you" (Matthew 6.16-18 NIV).

**Spiritual Benefit #7: Fasting Motivates us to Consume God's Word.**

We are both flesh and spirit. Many times, we keep our flesh well-fed, as our spirit wastes away. When we fast food from our bodies, we open the way for our spirit to consume God's Word like never before. Our starved spirit feasts on God's Word, supplying itself with needed sustenance and nutrients it desperately needs. Whenever we take something out of our life, we must fill it with something else. When we take food out, we fill it with the Bible. As we read the Bible, the reigning Spirit of God within us will teach, grow and transform us and the world around us.

> "But he said to them, 'I have food to eat that you know nothing about'" (John 4.32 NIV).

> "Jesus answered, It is written: 'Man shall not live on bread alone, but on every word that comes from the mouth of God'" (Matthew 4.4 NIV).

**First, the Water Fast: You Drink Only Water for a Set Time.**

This type of fasting is the most difficult because so much of our culture is wrapped around food and drinks. I like to do this fast for a few days as a lead into one of the other fasts. It's surprising how easy the other fasts are after a few days of having nothing but water.

**Second, the Juice Fast: You Drink Vegetable or Fruit Juice for a Set Time.**

The juice fast fills the body with needed nutrients and vitamins while still being able to flush away waste materials that have been stored in the body too long. Use a juicer at home or purchase fruit and vegetable juice without added sweeteners and preservatives.

**Third, the Intermittent Fast: You Fast Certain Times or Meals During the Day.**

Intermittent fasting allows you to skip meals in a day or fast on certain days in a week. For example, some people would prefer to fast breakfast and lunch and eat a healthy dinner. While others would prefer to have breakfast and lunch and skip dinner. Or some people prefer to fast from sunup to sundown, so they can have a small meal early before the day begins and a snack later after the sun has set. Also, some people choose to fast one day a week, like every Monday.

**Fourth, the Partial Fast: You Fast Certain Foods or Drinks**.

A partial fast allows you to take out certain foods from your diet. This fast is still difficult because we may crave our comfort foods and feel entitled to have them. This is why I like to start with a water fast first. It makes me appreciate the partial fast. The Daniel Diet is an example of the partial fast, which has you only eat fruits and vegetables. Another partial fast would be to take out all foods that are unhealthy for a time, like sodas, desserts and junk food.

**Fifth, the Calorie Restriction Fast: You Restrict Your Calories.**

Calorie restriction fast has you limit your calories for a day. For example, you can allow yourself to have 600 calories during the fast. You will still feel hungry, but you'll be able to satisfy the hunger a bit with a few nutritious snacks. The calories can be saved for one meal or spread throughout the day.

**Sixth, the Non-Food Fast: You Fast Something Other Than Food.**

A non-food fast is where you take something out of your life for a time that is not food. Some people like to fast social media, television, smoking, complaining or even worry.

**Seventh, the Reverse Fast: You Add Something into Your Life.**

Reverse fasting is where you add something to your life for a time. I like to do communion for a season, so I will add a time of prayer every day that includes the eucharist elements. Some people like to add additional Bible reading time, exercise, date nights or journaling. Whatever it is, you simply need to set the number of days you want to reverse fast and make sure you stay accountable to doing it every day.

# Day 4

## [2 TYPES OF SIGNS FROM GOD]

Asking God for signs to boost our faith can be a bit tricky. There are moments when we know what to do and asking for a sign for what we know is right shows a lack of trust in God's Word. However, there are moments in the Bible where people were faced with insurmountable odds, and God gladly gave them a sign to encourage their faith. People like Abraham, Gideon and even the world (when we were given the Star as a sign of the Messiah's arrival) have all received signs.

What I've learned about signs is that I don't ask for one unless I feel God's Spirit leading me or I'm really struggling with a new promise God has given me. I don't want to be like the religious leaders who demanded Jesus to show signs like He was a miracle-worker for hire (Matthew 16.1). I usually let the process of getting a sign to be initiated by God, and I try to stay sensitive to what He shows me every day.

In the book of Isaiah, King Ahaz is facing a devouring enemy that wants to destroy his kingdom, Judah. The odds against him are overwhelming, and God offers to give him a sign of confirmation.

> "Later, the Lord sent this message to King Ahaz: 'Ask the Lord your God for a sign of confirmation, Ahaz. Make it as difficult as you want—as high as heaven

or as deep as the place of the dead'" (Isaiah 7.10-11 NLT).

In his pride, however, King Ahaz rejects the sign and exhausts God's patience. So instead, the Prophet Isaiah gives the king a sign of the coming Messiah, Jesus Christ, which is the ultimate victory for all of us (Isaiah 7.14-15 NLT).

We will never know the exact reason King Ahaz rejected a sign from God, but we do know that he missed out on God's divine comfort and intervention in his life and situation.

**Two Kinds of Signs from God.**

God told King Ahaz that He would give him a sign "as high as heaven" or as "deep as the place of the dead." To me, this description represents the two types of signs that God offers us. Signs that are "as high as heaven" represent external signs. And signs that are "deep as the place of the dead" represent internal signs. I have experienced both these two types of signs, and they have been equally special and powerful in my life.

**External Sigs from God.**

External signs occur outside of us. They can happen in nature, through a sermon, in a book, from a friend, through a life situation, etc.

For example, I once stood on a deck overlooking a canal. I asked God why His promises seem to take so long to come to fruition. Suddenly, I noticed a large silver fish floating in the water. Then a seagull flew in from the east and swooped down to get it. He grabbed hold of it, but it was too big for him. He couldn't even get the fish out of the water. He gave up and flew away. Another seagull came in from the east and flew down to retrieve the fish. He flapped his wings several times with the fish in his grasp, but he finally let the fish drop back into the water. He couldn't carry the fish very long, so he decided to fly away. Finally, I felt the Holy Spirit prompt me to look west. I saw a huge seagull soar down over the canal with purpose. I don't know how he knew the fish was there, but he was determined to get it. He easily grabbed the fish and flew off.

What God showed me in that external sign was that I had to grow into the promises that He had for me. Promises come with both blessings and burdens, and He was maturing me and growing me stronger in Him.

**Internal Signs from God.**

Internal signs occur within us. These signs spring from the Living God within us, resonating in our own spirits in a supernatural way. They can occur in a dream, vision, a knowing, a feeling and an understanding that fills us.

For example, about two years ago, I got sailing certified with my husband. I used the information I learned as research for my fantasy fiction books, the *Violet Moon Series*. However, I was mainly supporting my husband's dream to sail. On the final day of our lessons, we had to sail to an island with the guidance of our captain and stay overnight on the boat. I became extremely ill while we were sailing. It was January and the weather was cold, and I felt terrible. When we finally made it to the port, I got medicine. But when I tried to sleep on the old boat in the tiny cabin, I

31

couldn't sleep. The boat kept rocking and banging against the dock. Everything was cold and moist. My throat burned and my body ached. I cried out to God. I didn't want to leave and disappoint my husband, but I had to get some sleep or I wouldn't be able to sail home the next day. I would lose my chance at getting sailing certified. Suddenly, in the midst of my pain and tears, sleep fell on me like a thick blanket. As I tucked myself into a deep slumber, I listened for a second. I still heard the noise. I still felt terrible. But God had blessed me with a supernatural sleep.

**Experiencing Signs of God.**

We want to be aware of how God's constantly communicating around and in us. He is there, desiring to be a part of our lives. He wants to encourage us when we are weak and give us space to stand strong in Him. If we are struggling, we can ask God to help us. He may want to give us an internal or external sign. We just have to be available and open to see and experience it. As we go to God, letting go of all the distractions that try to occupy our minds, hearts and day, we will be able to experience God more clearly and attain those internal and external signs He wants to give us to build our faith and give us peace.

# DAY 5

## [7 WAYS TO GET A MUSTARD SEED OF FAITH]

"I tell you, he will see that they get justice, and quickly. However, when the Son of Man comes, will he find faith on the earth?" (Luke 18.8 NIV).

**Faith to Move Mountains.**

Faith is another extremely powerful word. Jesus said all we need is a mustard seed of faith, and we can move mountains (Matthew 17.20). But why is something so small and assessable as a mustard seed seem so difficult to find and procure?

The devil knows that faith is simple, which is why he tries so hard to make it sound unattainable. But it's not. In fact, all it takes is a little trust, imagination, and action.

**Faith for a Wall Clock.**

I have a garage gym, and for a while now I've wanted a big wall clock with a second hand, so I can time my cardio calisthenics.

I finally bought my clock from Amazon, two-day shipping, and for the past few days, I keep looking at my wall completely expecting my clock to be there. I can envision it up there and my mind responds to my belief. I may not have seen it with my physical eyes, but everything inside of me is assured it's already there, so I respond out of that confidence. My faith is more real than my reality.

> "Now faith is confidence in what we hope for and assurance about what we do not see" (Hebrews 11.1 NIV).

**The Words of Faith Become Flesh.**

Words are a part of our language. What is language? It is the expression of all our thoughts, ideas, beliefs and feelings. It is the audible or visual expression of who we are. John says that Jesus is the Word, the ability for all things to express their existence through sound and movement. And what does the Word do? It becomes Flesh.

> "The Word became flesh and made his dwelling among us..." (John 1.14 NIV).

As the Word becomes Flesh, the words we speak become physical, but first, we must speak and move according to our belief.

Every time I look up at my wall to see my clock, I am expressing my belief through movement. Every time I declare that my clock is there, I am expressing my belief through sound. I am demonstrating faith in my words and actions.

**Faith in the Supernatural.**

Having faith in human promises is easy. I pay Amazon and believe the company will fulfill its order. Having faith in God's promises should be easy too, right? He is the Creator of the Universe and the Savior of our souls. Surely, if He can save us from eternity in hell, He can do anything.

We struggle with our faith because we don't fully believe God. This is a serious problem. We will never fulfill the dreams that God has for us unless we believe. The miracle of belief first occurs in us. Then it infiltrates our world.

> "Very truly I tell you, whoever believes in me will do the works I have been doing, and they will do even greater things than these, because I am going to the Father" (John 14.12 NIV)

If we say we have faith, and our words and actions don't follow suit, our faith is dead. Our words and actions must respond to our belief. If we are struggling to fully believe, we must ask God to help us with our unbelief. God wants us to believe, so He can fulfill the promises He has for us. Sometimes we must get our words and actions moving according to our promises to ignite our dead faith.

> "In the same way, faith by itself, if it is not accompanied by action, is dead" (James 2.17 NIV).

**What You Can Do Ignite Your Faith.**

If God has given you promises, you can do everything in the natural to achieve those promises. But all your work will be fruitless unless the miracle of belief is birthed within you. Don't forget. Faith is small and assessable, or Jesus wouldn't have compared it to a mustard seed. You don't need a truckload of seeds. You just need one tiny seed to move a mountain – one seed of faith planted inside of you to

Reframing | Alisa Hope Wagner

unleash your destiny. But how? Here is a list of what I am doing to ignite my faith.

**First, Get Faith by Knowing Your Father.**

If you don't know Who God is, you won't trust His words for your life. Intimacy is an inside job. Take time every day to really get to know your Father. Intimacy takes time, so don't try to rush it. Just seek Him, and your relationship with God will grow.

**Second, Get Faith by Reading Your Bible.**

If Jesus is the Word, then His Spirit is the Bible. Drink from it every day. Even if you don't feel like your Bible reading is doing anything at first, keep consuming it. Your spiritual saturation will start to show, and it will fuel your faith.

**Third, Get Faith by Praying All the Time.**

Start to pray about everything. What you eat, what you drink, what you wear, where you go....it may sound funny, but include God in all your decisions, not just the big ones. When you start seeing God come through for you in the little things, you'll be more likely to trust Him for the bigger things.

**Fourth, Get Faith by Speaking Your Promises.**

Fight doubt by speaking faith-filled words out loud. Fill the atmosphere with every one of God's promises. You may sound nonsensical at first, but that's okay. God's plans are bigger than you. He can and will accomplish everything He sets out to do. He just needs your belief! Don't speak your

36

reality. Speak God's reality. Unleash what's in heaven onto earth with your words.

**Fifth, Get Faith by Moving in Trust.**

Your decisions and actions every day should be dictated by your belief. If you are believing God for something, you want to move in the direction of that promise. You may not be able to accomplish the full vision of your destiny alone, but you can at least do your part. Make sure you are responding according to belief, not doubt.

**Sixth, Get Faith by Not Giving Up.**

God is preparing you to carry the burden of your promises. This may take time, especially if your promises are big. Don't quit. Learn to wait. The process is part of the promise. The longer the wait, the sweeter the victory. Don't lose heart. Learn to enjoy each day as a person pregnant with destiny. The birth will come according to God's timing.

**Seventh, Get Faith by Binding and Loosing it.**

Seek God's will, learn His promises in His Word, then forbid (bind) and loose (permit) according to His Kingdom Plan. Is there something in your life that is not of God? Forbid it. Is there something missing from your life that God wants you to have? Permit it. You have power as a child of God. Learn to use that power to accomplish all God has for you. And when you bind something, make sure you loose something, as well.

> "Truly I tell you, whatever you bind on earth will be bound in heaven, and whatever you loose on

earth will be loosed in heaven" (Matthew 18.18 NIV).

# DAY 6

# [4 WAYS TO AN AWESOME MARRIAGE USING WORDS]

**You can have an awesome marriage simply by using your words.**

> "Gentle words are a tree of life..." (Proverbs 15.4 NLT).

As an introverted, shy person who struggled with insecurity, I've had to learn to shape my marriage with words. I married my high school sweetheart, and we've been married for twenty-two years. Wise words, I have found, are one of the easiest and most profound ways to cultivate an awesome marriage.

Words truly have the power of life and death, and many people do not know how to use their tongue to create their dream marriage. But once you realize that words literally can dictate your marital bliss, you will begin to use words to build an awesome marriage.

> "The tongue can bring death or life; Those who love to talk will reap the consequences" (Proverbs 18.21 NLT).

**First, Stop Bad Talking Yourself.**

If you are unable to use words to build yourself up, it will be very difficult to build up others or your marriage. The

Bible says to love others as you love yourself (Mark 12.31). So guess what? If you don't love yourself in a healthy way, you will not love others in a healthy way. You must make a conscious decision to stop speaking negatively about yourself. Read what the Bible has to say about you.

- You have been wonderfully made (Psalm 139.14).
- God loved you so much that He died for you (Romans 5.8).
- You are royalty (1 Peter 2.9).
- You have purpose (Ephesian 1.11).

There is nothing wrong with correcting yourself and learning from your mistakes, but under no circumstances should you bad-talk your body, your intelligence, your feelings and your purpose. When you bad-talk the creation, you bad-talk the Creator. God is perfect and holy, and Jesus has redeemed us of all through His Work on the Cross. You are beautiful and valuable because God made you, and He doesn't make mistakes.

**Second, Realize Your Spouse is Not Perfect.**

If you start focusing on all the negative aspects of your spouse, you will verbalize them more. You will literally become obsessed with tiny details that don't matter in the long run. Instead, look at all the amazing things your spouse does for you and your family. We tend to place less value on the things we have taken for granted, so open your eyes to all the good your spouse does and verbalize them. Words have power. Even if you only see a little good at first, start speaking them out loud. The enemy hates it when we see the good in people. Satan would much rather we focus on the negative because that's what he does. Use your words to fight back.

God loves your marriage, so use your words to protect it.

- Make a list of things your spouse does well and speak them out loud for all to hear.
- Tell God how thankful you are for your spouse and marriage.
- Fill your home with the aroma of sweet words to replace negative ones.
- Pray before speaking correction to ensure the Holy Spirit is guiding your speech.
- "Kind words are like honey—sweet to the soul and healthy for the body" (Proverbs 16.24 NLT).

**Third, Surround Yourself with Godly Influences.**

Even if you didn't grow up in a healthy home with a healthy example of marriage, you can still learn. God is awesome at creating something new (Isaiah 43.19) and transforming what was done for harm into your good.

> "As for you, you meant evil against me, but God meant it for good..." (Genesis 50.20 ESV).

God has His best design for your life, but you won't get there without work. Roll up your sleeves and learn and grow. Life is too short to accept mediocrity. It may feel uncomfortable at first, but you can be the loving husband or wife God created you to be. Pour energy and effort into your marriage and make it your top priority. Your marriage is worth fighting for.

Surround yourself with people who have healthy, happy marriages, so you can have a blueprint of their words for your own marital success. You can watch how they interact. Listen to the words they use. And ask them questions to help guide you and your spouse.

- Find a couple who has the marriage you want and ask to be mentored by them.
- Consume Christian resources (read and listen to positive words) on how to have a great marriage.
- If your marriage has serious strongholds, go to a Christian counselor for guidance.
- Pray. Prayer reaches into the supernatural and influences the natural. Pray for your spouse and marriage daily.

"Wise words are like deep waters; wisdom flows from the wise like a bubbling brook" (Proverbs 18.4 NLT).

# DAY 7

# [5 KEYS TO UNLOCK YOUR SUPERPOWER]

**Praying Out Loud is Your Superpower.**

The Holy Spirit has been impressing on me to pray out loud. I feel its importance. Praying out loud is a power I need to tap into. When I asked God about it, He gave me an image of Gandalf from *Lord of the Rings*. I saw Gandalf speaking his words out loud to change the circumstances around him. Gandalf used his words for good to fight evil. But he had to cast them into the situation. Like Gandalf, we too can project our prayers into areas of faith.

> "Faith shows the reality of what we hope for; it is the evidence of things we cannot see" (Hebrews 11.1 NLT).

**Praying Out Loud by Faith.**

I have many areas of faith, and I want to see my circumstances change. I want to fight evil and be a voice of good to the world around me. My words can create supernatural events that point to Jesus. Praying out loud is a declaration of faith to myself and the world. I know my faith can move mountains because God's Word says so (Matthew 17.20). I want to wield my superpower to move the obstacles trying to block God's Promises. Praying out loud helps us to tangibly hear our declarations, so our faith will be boosted.

43

"So then faith comes by hearing, and hearing by the word of God" (Romans 10.17 NKJV).

**5 Keys to Unlocking Your Superpower by Praying Out Loud.**

Praying out loud has drastically transformed my prayer life. Before I sometimes prayed passively in my heart. Now I pray out loud like I am in a courtroom standing before the Judge. I know that the Judge has all the power, authority and resources in the universe. I want to fill His throne room with words of faith and belief. I know my words are my superpower that can shape my circumstances. I see God's promises in the supernatural by faith, and I use my words like tethers to pull them into the natural.

"You can pray for anything, and if you have faith, you will receive it" (Matthew 21.22 NLT).

**Key 1 to Unlock Your Superpower: Praying Out Loud in the Spirit.**

We must see ourselves as the righteousness of God through Jesus Christ. Our prayers won't be heard based on our own merit. They are heard based on Jesus alone. We magnify Jesus' perfection, so our flaws diminish. We can come boldly to the throne of God because of Jesus' Finished Work on the Cross (Hebrews 4.16). We are seated with Christ at the right hand of God (Ephesians 2.6 & Colossians 3.1). Our words have power because they are covered by the redeeming Blood of Jesus Christ. When we pray out loud, we can be God's mouthpiece to the world.

"Pray in the Spirit at all times and on every occasion. Stay alert and be persistent in your prayers for all believers everywhere" (Ephesians 6.18 NLT).

**Key 2 to Unlock Your Superpower: Praying Out Loud in Jesus' Name.**

Jesus is the most powerful name in all the universe (Philippians 2.9-11). The enemy must bow to that name. The enemies in your life and circumstances are weakened and destroyed by that name. We can pray the name of Jesus out loud into all situations. It is only by the Name of Jesus that heaven can hear our prayers. All our words hinge on His name. Praying out loud in the name of Jesus adds the seal of God onto our words. They will be received!

"You can ask for anything in my name, and I will do it, so that the Son can bring glory to the Father. Yes, ask me for anything in my name, and I will do it" (John 14.13-14 NLT).

**Key 3 to Unlock Your Superpower: Praying Out Loud for God's Promises.**

We must first know God's promises before we pray them out loud. We don't have to be confused about what to pray for. The Bible is full of God's promises for all areas of our life. When we ask God for His Kingdom Plan, we can pray that plan back to Him. And when the obstacles try to prevent God's plan from coming to fruition, we can pray out loud believing for a miracle. God loves to show His glory in our lives, and He does this by defying all odds. Nothing for God is impossible (Matthew 19.26).

"For all of God's promises have been fulfilled in Christ with a resounding 'Yes!' And through Christ, our 'Amen' (which means 'Yes') ascends to God for his glory" (2 Corinthians 1.20 NLT).

**Key 4 to Unlock Your Superpower: Praying Out Loud with Detail.**

God is in the details. When we are believing by faith, the details of His promises will boost our faith. We can pray out loud very specifically about what we are believing for. God loves us and designed us as a one-of-a-kind masterpiece (Ephesians 2.10). We each have our own unique perspective on the world. Our specific prayers spoken out loud show God that we value how He created us. They also are a sign that we are invested in what He is doing in our lives.

"And since we know he hears us when we make our requests, we also know that he will give us what we ask for" (1 John 5.15 NLT).

**Key 5 To Unlock Your Superpower: Praying Out Loud by Faith.**

Words are meaningless unless we truly believe them. Many times, we are believing in promises that seem dead in the natural. We must choose to believe by faith not sight (2 Corinthians 5.7). When we pray out loud, we are putting action into our belief. We are telling God and the world that we believe God is stronger than our situation. His promises are already set in stone. Praying out loud is a superpower that helps us wield God's authority in our lives. Our words dipped in belief will change the world around us.

"And it is impossible to please God without faith. Anyone who wants to come to him must believe that God exists and that he rewards those who sincerely seek him" (Hebrews 11.6 NLT).

# DAY 8

## [7 WAYS TO BRING GOD WITH YOU]

**Bringing God with you every moment is a choice.**

Moses understood that no matter how much he learned and grew as a leader, he could not do it alone. He could not accomplish the great things that God had for him without God's help. Moses told God: "If Your presence does not go, don't make us go up from here" (Exodus 33.15 HSCB). Moses would rather stay and wait than move without God's presence.

When we begin to rely on our own strength, we will forge ahead without asking for God's guidance in the matter. If God doesn't go with us, we will have to support the results of our choices on our own. Eventually, our strength and resources will run dry, and we'll wonder why everything seems so hard.

Moses saw his need for divine help. He had a million plus people with all sorts of talents and resources at his disposal, but even with all that support, Moses knew they wouldn't be enough. Moses could have asked God for more resources, more connections, more wisdom or more influence (none of which are wrong requests), but he got down to the core problem: nothing valuable and eternal is possible without God.

We are in desperate need of a Savior. We are nothing without God. All the talent, money and influence in the world doesn't make a bit of difference if God is not with us. We can't do it alone. Once we realize our complete dependence on God and His saving grace through Jesus Christ, we won't make any decisions or take any actions unless we know that God is going with us.

When we finally begin to rely on our limitless God, He can do the miraculous through us and our efforts, and everyone will know that He is with us. Whatever we do and wherever we go, we want to ask God to join us.

> "The Lord replied, 'Listen, I am making a covenant with you in the presence of all your people. I will perform miracles that have never been performed anywhere in all the earth or in any nation. And all the people around you will see the power of the Lord—the awesome power I will display for you'" (Exodus 34.10 NLT).

**Way 1: Bring God with You by Seeing Your Need for Him.**

God is the creator of all things. He dwells outside of time, and He sees our victory. He has unlimited resources ready to help us achieve His will, but we must rely on Him. We may want to rely on people and things that we can see and touch, but only God can fulfill His plans in and through us.

> "Jesus looked at them intently and said, 'Humanly speaking, it is impossible. But with God everything is possible'" (Matthew 19.26 NLT).

**Way2: Bring God with You by Not Moving Right Away.**

Fools act on impulse. Once we realize we need God, we will less likely jump ahead of Him. We will wait for Him to give us the green light, so we can have His supernatural power flowing in our actions. Waiting on God's timing is one of the most difficult disciplines to learn, yet the most powerful.

> "Wise people think before they act; fools don't—and even brag about their foolishness" (Proverbs 13.16 NLT).

**Way 3: Bring God with You by Relying on Him for Everything.**

God's system of doing things is very different than the world's system. When we rely on human understanding, we may miss all that God has planned for us. God sometimes only shows us a few steps ahead because the full picture won't make sense to us. But we can trust God knows what He's doing. We can always rely on God's faithfulness in ways that we may not yet comprehend.

> "'My thoughts are nothing like your thoughts,' says the Lord. 'And my ways are far beyond anything you could imagine. For just as the heavens are higher than the earth, so my ways are higher than your ways and my thoughts higher than your thoughts'" (Isaiah 55.8-9 NLT).

**Way 4: Bring God with You by Praying Every Day.**

Seeking God every morning places our feet firmly on His path for our life. Whether He wants us to wait or go, we can trust that we are right where He wants us to be every day. Then the days of our obedient waiting and going will accumulate, and we will be directly on His overarching Kingdom Plan. However, we must listen for Him and commune with Him daily.

> "Listen to my voice in the morning, LORD. Each morning I bring my requests to you and wait expectantly" (Psalm 5.3 NLT).

**Way 5: Bring God with You by Praying about Everything.**

Prayer is our weapon against fear. When our thoughts and actions are motivated by fear, we are going in the wrong direction away from God's will. Making choices out of a spirit of fear leads to disaster because we start making decisions outside of God's protection. When we feel worry creep up, we need to make room for more God and replace fear with faith.

> "Don't worry about anything; instead, pray about everything. Tell God what you need, and thank him for all he has done. Then you will experience God's peace, which exceeds anything we can understand. His peace will guard your hearts and minds as you live in Christ Jesus" (Philippians 4.6-7 NLT).

**Way 6: Bring God with You by Reading Scripture Every Day.**

Whether we read our Bible, read Christian literature and/or listen to sermons, we can drink from the Word of God daily. The Bible literally is the Person of Jesus in written form (John 1). The resurrection power of Jesus Christ is in the Word. Take from this power as often as possible.

> "I also pray that you will understand the incredible greatness of God's power for us who believe him. This is the same mighty power that raised Christ from the dead and seated him in the place of honor at God's right hand in the heavenly realms" (Ephesians 1.19-20 NLT).

**Way 7: Bring God with You by Allowing Jesus to Renew You.**

We will never be perfect. Even if God is going with us, we will sometimes stumble and fall. We can either fixate on our mistakes or understand that the Blood of Jesus is constantly at work cleansing and perfecting us. Our sins are gone. We have been redeemed. God's corrections are drenched in love and approval.

> "But if we are living in the light, as God is in the light, then we have fellowship with each other, and the blood of Jesus, his Son, cleanses us from all sin" (1 John 1.7 NLT).

# DAY 9

# [7 PRACTICES TO MAKE GOD REAL IN THE HOME]

I have a family of six — me, my husband, our three kids and God. My husband and I are very intentional about making God a real, tangible member of our family. We don't simply just talk about God, we demonstrate Him in relevant ways, so our kids can truly know Him and learn to do life with Him. Our two sons and daughter will learn about having a relationship with God by first watching their parents. We make Him real in our home. How can we allow God to be a relevant part of our Family?

**First, We Talk about Our Experiences to Make God Real in Our Home.**

We describe what God is teaching us in the Bible. We share how God showed us something through nature. My husband and I are constantly sharing real ways God is speaking to us. We chat to each other in front of our kids, and we include them in our conversations about God.

> "They triumphed over him by the blood of the Lamb and by the word of their testimony..." (Revelation 12.11 NIV).

**Second, We Pray Aloud to Make God Real in Our Home.**

At first, praying in front of my children felt uncomfortable. But I knew if they didn't learn it from me, who then would they learn from? So, I began praying out loud when they were very young. I prayed for the people in the ambulance who passed us by on the street. I prayed for the tragedies on the news. I prayed for family and friends who were struggling. And I prayed for them about every pain, worry, struggle and heartache they had. Plus, my husband and I pray for them at bedtime every night.

> "Rejoice always, pray continually, give thanks in all circumstances; for this is God's will for you in Christ Jesus" (1 Thessalonians 5.16-18 NIV).

**Third, We Read the Bible Every Morning to Make God Real in our Home.**

We either read from the Bible or grab a devotional and read it while the kids eat breakfast. Right now we are reading my one-year devotional, *Slay the Day*, and the kids are hearing truth spoken over them. They hear God's Words, and that makes Him more real.

> "Keep this Book of the Law always on your lips; meditate on it day and night, so that you may be careful to do everything written in it. Then you will be prosperous and successful" (Joshua 1.8 NIV).

**Fourth, We Confess our Wrongs and Apologize to Make God Real in Our Home.**

There is no such thing as a perfect parent. The best we can be is flawed but perfected in grace. God can change a heart, but the heart must be willing. We demonstrate humility to our kids, so they can see God tangibly working in us.

> "Therefore confess your sins to each other and pray for each other so that you may be healed. The prayer of a righteous person is powerful and effective" (James 5.16 NIV).

**Fifth, We Explain the Trinity to Make God Real in Our Home.**

The Trinity of God can be confusing, but I explain to my kids this simple analogy. I tell them that their father is 1) a dad, 2) a husband and 3) a doctor. He is the same person, but he relates to others in different ways, depending on what he's doing and their needs. The same goes for God. He is real and interacts with us in distinct ways.

> "May the grace of the Lord Jesus Christ, and the love of God, and the fellowship of the Holy Spirit be with you all" (2 Corinthians 13.14 NIV).

**Sixth, We Tell Our Kids to Ask God to Make Him Real in Our Home.**

Sometimes, my husband and I don't have the answers. When our kids struggle, we pray with them. However, we always suggest that they pray to God for themselves. Listening to God is difficult at first, but like any relationship, intimacy takes effort, consistency and time. He will become more real in their lives as they learn to pray one-on-one with Him.

> "Call to me and I will answer you and tell you great and unsearchable things you do not know" (Jeremiah 33.3 NIV).

**Seventh, We Surround our Kids with Christian Influences to Make God Real in Our Home.**

My husband and I attend church weekly. This ensures that our kids are influenced by other Christians. We want our kids to be involved in another ministry outside of the home. Church allows them to experience a tangible God from other perspectives. Also, we open our home to our church's small groups, and the kids attend church youth events. Simply staying consistent in showing up to church allows our family to experience God in fresh ways.

> "And let us not neglect our meeting together, as some people do, but encourage one another, especially now that the day of his return is drawing near" (Hebrews 10.25 NLT).

# DAY 10

# [3 BENEFITS OF SUBMISSION IN MARRIAGE]

**Submission in Marriage is the Glue.**

> "And further, submit to one another out of reverence for Christ" (Ephesians 5.21 NLT).

As Christians, men and women both have the Holy Spirit dwelling within us. Jesus died for each of us. We are all royal priests through Christ (1 Peter 2.9). Although men and women have equal value, we each have unique roles of submission within marriage. These roles have been established by God for the profit of the husband, wife, marriage and family.

Both men and women are submitted to some sort of leadership in life according to their age, their careers and their family status. Submission is not an ugly, domineering thing. Submission is literally what binds, protects and raises a ministry, business, family and, yes, a marriage. In fact, Jesus submitted Himself unto death and now sits at the right hand of God (Hebrews 10.12). His submission is what binds, protects and raises us, the Church.

> "And being found in appearance as a man, he humbled himself by becoming obedient to death— even death on a cross!" (Philippians 2.8 NIV).

Submission is like a glue that draws diverse people together, so that God can catapult them into higher levels without everything falling apart. Nothing great can happen without submission. Jesus' life was a demonstration of that truth.

**Submission in Marriage Binds.**

A woman's role as wife is different from her role as employee, boss, owner, prophet, teacher, leader, etc. In all other roles outside of marriage, she will have points of leadership and submission just like anyone else. Same is true for a man's role as husband. His submission in marriage will look different than the other roles he fulfills outside of the home.

According to Ephesians 5.21, both wife and husband are submitted to each other. However, their submissions are not identical, they are complements. When the man and woman make their marriage vows, they commit to being united as one just as the Church is united with Christ. They are now husband and wife. A mysterious and supernatural binding occurs that only submission in Christ can keep together.

> "As the Scriptures say, 'A man leaves his father and mother and is joined to his wife, and the two are united into one.' This is a great mystery, but it is an illustration of the way Christ and the church are one" (Ephesians 5.31-32 NLT).

**The Wife is Submitted to Her Husband as to the Lord.**

> "Wives, be subject to your own husbands, as [a service] to the Lord. For the husband is head of the wife, as Christ is head of the church, Himself being the Savior of the body" (Ephesians 5.22-23 AMP).

The wife trusts her husband because he is the authority God has placed in her life. This authority is for her protection and blessing. Yes, no one is perfect and her husband may make mistakes (as will she), but God is more than capable of turning all things for her good (Romans 8.28 NIV).

**The Husband is Submitted to His Wife as to the Church**.

> "Husbands, love your wives [seek the highest good for her and surround her with a caring, unselfish love], just as Christ also loved the church and gave Himself up for her" (Ephesians 5.25 AMP).

The husband is head over the family, like Christ is head over the Church. And the husband should willingly give his life for his wife, like Christ gave His life for the Church. His submission is to the care, protection and love of his wife. And like Christ, this submission leads to the death of his own selfish desires (Galatians 5.24).

**Submission in the Marriage Protects.**

The wife protects her marriage by submitting herself to her husband's authority. For any institution to work, there must be a system of authority. God is the ultimate authority, and the husband responds to God's directive. The husband then is expected to protect and provide for his wife and family with his everything. When a wife submits to her husband's authority, she will be protected, blessed and cared for by

God and her husband. She submits herself as to the Lord, and her life will have a holy ease of being yoked to Jesus (Matthew 11.29-30 NLT).

The husband protects his marriage by submitting his life to the care of his wife. The husband cherishes his wife—even if it means giving up his own life. This is the ultimate sign of responsibility—protection unto death. This death doesn't always have to be literal. Metaphorically, the husband dies to his own needs in order to protect and care for his wife. When a husband loves his wife, he is loving himself and his marriage (Ephesians 5.28 NLT).

The submission of both husband and wife ensures the protection of the marriage. Healthy, God-ordained submission causes the husband and wife to cling together. When the husband and wife say the words, "I do," they are declaring to themselves, to the world and to God that the needs of the marriage now usurp their individual needs. But as the wife serves her husband as unto the Lord and the husband serves his wife as unto the Church, they will find their own needs being met by God and each other.

> "And my God will meet all your needs according to the riches of his glory in Christ Jesus" (Philippians 4.19 NIV).

**Submission in Marriage Raises Up.**

When the husband submits as to the Church and the wife submits as to the Lord, the marriage rises above all others. The glory of God can shine through a marriage submitted to God's ordained authority. The marriage becomes a united front that cannot be divided. This is a unique submission of wife and husband, not seen anywhere else in all the world. Indeed, it is a mystery to people who don't know or trust God and His ways. But God does things beyond our understanding, and His system is not our own (Isaiah 58.8-9 NIV). When a husband and wife are firmly glued together, God can launch them into greatness that shines His glory to the world.

> "Rise up and shine, for your light has come. The shining-greatness of the Lord has risen upon you" (Isaiah 60.1 NLV).

# DAY 11

## [5 WAYS TO SURRENDER: LETTING GO TO GOD]

Surrendering to God is showing complete faith in Him and belief in His promises. Just like a child, we can walk in freedom from worries. We simply must choose to trust God for everything. If we can trust God for our salvation through Jesus Christ, we can trust Him for our daily needs and desires.

> "Truly I tell you, unless you change and become like little children, you will never enter the kingdom of heaven" (Matthew 18.3 NIV).

**What to Surrender.**

Everything. Surrender is literally giving up all control. It is telling God that we are not big enough to deal with our worries, and He must take over. When we finally let go of all our worries, we give God room to wield His mighty arm in our lives. When our hands are weak and tired, God's hands are strong and powerful!

> "Powerful is your arm! Strong is your hand! Your right hand is lifted high in glorious strength" (Psalm 89.13 NLT).

**How to Surrender.**

Surrendering control is a daily, moment-by-moment choice. Like every discipline in life, we must learn to surrender and give it to God. The enemy seeks every new day to cloud our mind with worries, doubts and fears. The devil wants there to be no room left for God in our lives. Surrendering to God becomes a lifestyle of daily giving it all to Him.

Whenever negative thoughts seek to invade our space, we must cut them and give them to God immediately. God's mercies are new every morning, so what happened yesterday, last year or a decade ago is completely gone. Carrying the past around will only take up space meant for God's goodness, grace and favor. Renewing our mind in Christ means letting go of all the burdens He died to take from us.

> "The steadfast love of the Lord never ceases; his mercies never come to an end; they are new every morning; great is your faithfulness" (Lamentations 3.22-23 ESV).

**First thing to Let Go – Control.**

Control is the hardest thing to give up because without it we feel vulnerable. But we do not need to worry. God is already in control. We need to recognize His authority and move aside to let Him lead. He is the Creator of the universe, so we can trust Him with each day. Letting go is scary at first, but the freedom in our minds and hearts will be worth it.

> "And we know that for those who love God all things work together for good, for those who are called according to his purpose" (Romans 8.28 ESV).

**Second Thing to Let Go – Worry.**

Worry adds not a single day to our lives. In fact, worry oppresses us every second. Worry can literally affect not only our minds and hearts but our bodies too. Worry does absolutely nothing positive. Surrender worry to God and watch your life float in His favor.

> "Don't worry about anything; instead, pray about everything. Tell God what you need, and thank him for all he has done" (Philippians 4.6 NLT).

**Third Thing to Let Go – Money.**

We tend to hold tightly to our money. However, God wants to take the reins of our money. Money can become an idol if we place it before God. God wants to bless us, so we need to put our finances in their proper place: In God's hands. God will take care of us. We simply need to surrender our money and obey His leading.

> "Keep your life free from love of money, and be content with what you have, for he has said, 'I will never leave you nor forsake you'" (Hebrews 13.5 ESV).

**Fourth Thing to Let Go – Relationships.**

Surrendering to God's sovereign will in our relationships shows that we trust Him with the people we care about. We can't possibly be everyone's savior and hero, but Jesus can. He died because He loves all of us, including the people most precious to us. We can do everything in our power to love and care for those entrusted to us and trust God with the rest.

> "And if God cares so wonderfully for wildflowers that are here today and thrown into the fire tomorrow, he will certainly care for you. Why do you have so little faith?" (Matthew 6.30 NLT).

**Fifth Thing to Let Go – The Future.**

We can only change one day at a time. Living in the future robs us of the joy of today. Each day is a gift, and we miss it when we allow our minds to dwell on all the unknowns. We can trust God with our future, so we can focus on today. Trying to control the future is like trying to control the wind. Contentment in today will prevent our eyes from wandering off to tomorrow.

> "Therefore do not worry about tomorrow, for tomorrow will worry about itself" (Matthew 6.34 NIV).

# DAY 12

## [7 BLESSINGS TO SPEAKING WISE WORDS]

The words we speak in the flesh are filled with discontent, hate, jealousy, fear and despair. The words we speak in the spirit are filled with love, joy, hope, encouragement and truth. Jesus died to forgive us of all our sins. When we speak words in our flesh, Jesus' blood instantly erases them. When we speak words in the spirit, they will fill heaven's reality. Because these wise words are rooted in the Vine of Christ, they will surround us in heaven for eternity. For this reason, we want to replace flesh-spoken words with spirit-spoken words because only they are eternal.

> "I am the true vine, and my Father is the gardener. He cuts off every branch in me that bears no fruit, while every branch that does bear fruit he prunes so that it will be even more fruitful" (John 15.1-2 NIV).

Speaking negative words in the flesh is a very difficult habit to overcome. However, there is a solution: Love. When we filter our attention on others through love instead of judgment, we will speak wise words. We are social creatures, and we like to contemplate the world and the people in it. The desire to embrace others with our thoughts can be extremely beneficial when submitted to the leadership and guidance of the Holy Spirit. Instead of using our words to destroy, we can use our wise words to build ourselves and others up.

"Therefore encourage one another and build each other up, just as in fact you are doing" (1 Thessalonians 5.11 NIV).

## The Blessings of Speaking Wise Words.

When we have the urge to speak in our flesh, our hearts and minds are telling us there is new information to analyze and assimilate into our understanding. In a moment, we have a choice of two paths—blessings or curses. We can show mercy and offer a blessing to others or we can show judgment and offer a curse. The choice is all ours. We can speak eternal words of the spirit or empty words of the flesh.

The Bible has a lot to say about our words. When we fully understand the power of the tongue, we will be very careful about what we think and speak. The tongue is literally a weapon that can be used for good or evil. There is not an in-between. When we speak words in the flesh, our tongue is used for evil. When we speak words in the spirit, our tongue is used for good. Once we learn to wield this weapon for good, we can reap the benefits.

## 7 Blessings When We Speak Wise Words.

Not only can we bless others with our words, but we can also bless ourselves. The Bible gives us 7 promises that are unleashed as we replace flesh-spoken words with spirit-spoken words. When we choose to bless others, we literally bless ourselves. When we choose to curse others, we in turn curse ourselves. We can transform our talk into a force for good by speaking life. As we get better at replacing negative words with wise words, our life will experience massive positive results.

> "Today I have given you the choice between life and death, between blessings and curses..." (Deuteronomy 30.19 NLT).

**Blessing 1: We will Enjoy Life More.**

We don't realize it, but when we speak negative words about others, we too become covered with negativity. However, if we learn to transform our words of judgment to words of mercy, our days will become good and joyful. We will not be bogged down by the words of destruction we have spoken aloud.

> "If you want joy in your life and have happy days, keep your tongue from saying bad things and your lips from talking bad about others" (1 Peter 3.10 NLV).

**Blessing 2: We Will Always Have an Answer.**

We may not know everything, but God certainly does. When He can trust us with our words, He will open up His wisdom and release it on our lives. The void left behind after we stop criticizing will be replaced by God's righteous words of wisdom.

> "Let your conversation be gracious and attractive so that you will have the right response for everyone" (Colossians 4.6 NLT).

**Blessing 3: We Will Have Close Friends.**

Friendships are a choice, and they take work, but they can greatly enrich and bless our lives and keep us on the right track. People are not perfect, and our friends will make mistakes. If we choose to forgive instead of complaining about the transgression, our relationships will prosper. And when we make a mistake, mercy can then be extended to us.

> "Love prospers when a fault is forgiven, but dwelling on it separates close friends" (Proverbs 17.9 NLT).

**Blessing 4: We Will Have Healing**.

Our words will not only bring healing to others, but they can also bring healing to us. The power of Jesus Christ is found in mercy. When we speak words of mercy in prayer instead of criticism, we are surrounding ourselves and others in an atmosphere of healing. Our bodies, minds and hearts will all benefit from the healing power around us.

> "Some people make cutting remarks, but the words of the wise bring healing" (Proverbs 12.18 NLT).

**Blessing 5: We Will Have Satisfaction.**

Speaking words in the flesh becomes a fire that can't be quenched (Proverbs 26.20). We will stress ourselves out overthinking about people and situations, and our hearts will be robbed of satisfaction. When we fill the atmosphere with negative words, we become the person speaking out of turn in the courtroom who will eventually be removed. When we choose to speak wise words, our words will be heard by the Judge Whose verdict is final.

69

"Wise words satisfy like a good meal; the right words bring satisfaction" (Proverbs 18.20 NLT).

**Blessing 6: We Will Have Peace.**

No money in the world can buy true peace. Peace comes to us each day because we replace negative words with wise words. Our words can free us or enslave us. When we choose to speak words of the spirit, we surround ourselves, our homes and our relationships with God's unending peace. How simple it is to have peace. All we need to do is learn to speak wise words.

"He who watches over his mouth and his tongue keeps his soul from troubles" (Proverbs 21.23 NLV).

**Blessing 7: We Will Have Life.**

The Bible says that the power of life and death is in our words. This realization should make us only want to speak life. When we speak wise words, we are literally pouring life onto us and those around us. We can reap fruits of blessings or curses. The choice is ours, and all we have to do is use our tongue to speak words of the spirit.

"The tongue can bring death or life; those who love to talk will reap the consequences" (Proverbs 18.21 NLT).

**How Can We Start Using Wise Words?**

When we see something that we don't like in someone, we should first go to God in prayer. We can pray for that person and the situation and ask God for clarity. That way we will have stopped ourselves from speaking words in the flesh, and we won't reap the negative fruit they produce. Before we speak to anyone else about our thoughts, we should always turn to God first. The Holy Spirit will convict us if we are showing judgment instead of mercy.

If there is a person or situation that is truly unfair, God is our Judge, not us. He is our Redeemer and our Counselor. We can tattle on others to God, and trust that He will accomplish both His justice and mercy in us and others. When we realize that we have been saved from a life separated from God because of the mercy of Jesus on the cross, it will be easier for us to offer mercy to others. So before speaking, let us choose wise words.

> "Do not judge others, and you will not be judged. For you will be treated as you treat others. The standard you use in judging is the standard by which you will be judged" (Matthew 7.1-2 NLT).

# DAY 13

## [10 ENCOURAGING BIBLE VERSES FOR WEIGHT LOSS]

There are a lot of encouraging verses that can help us with our weight loss journey. However, I have found that these 10 verses empower us the most by offering motivation that we truly need without guilt or shame. Shame is probably the number one stronghold that prevents people from losing weight, and it does not inspire change. Jesus loves us into transformation, while the world would seek to condemn us. Guilt is not lasting nor loving.

We can lose weight while still maintaining the joy of each day. We can lose weight knowing that we have the power of the Holy Spirit on our side. God sees the best in us, and He wants to bring that person to completion. We are not alone. We are all in the process of growing, changing and becoming our best selves. It is never too late to transform our lives. In fact, a new turn off the beaten path may be just what we need to revitalize the beauty of life.

**Below are My 10 Encouraging Verses for Weight Loss.**

I also offer a short description of how each verse can be applied to your weight loss journey. I pray that the God of the universe shows Himself so powerfully in your life through the grace of Jesus Christ. Your weight loss journey will be victorious as you lean on God.

**Weight Loss Verse 1: You Can Do All Things.**

72

> "I can do all this through him who gives me strength" (Philippians 4.13 NIV).

This verse is well known but rarely applied. If it is in the Bible, it is a promise that cannot be broken. God does not lie. If He has called you to lose weight, you can do it! Just believe that He will give you the grace you need each day on your weight loss journey. Change is most difficult in the beginning, but Jesus has already won the victory for you. He promises that you CAN DO ALL THINGS, including losing weight.

**Weight Loss Verse 2: God's Power is Made Perfect.**

> "But he said to me, 'My grace is sufficient for you, for my power is made perfect in weakness.' Therefore I will boast all the more gladly about my weaknesses, so that Christ's power may rest on me" (2 Corinthians 12.9 NIV).

We can trust that God's power will be strong in our weakness. We don't have to be embarrassed by our weaknesses. In fact, it is our weaknesses that cause us to lean on God and His strength. If we were "perfect" at everything, we would be tempted to rely solely on ourselves. Our weaknesses are not a curse. They are a gift because they enable us to put our faith and hope in God and allow His strength to shine in our lives. We can look at our weight loss as a chance for God's power to be made perfect in our lives.

**Weight Loss Verse 3: No Temptation will Overtake You.**

"No temptation has overtaken you except what is common to mankind. And God is faithful; he will not let you be tempted beyond what you can bear. But when you are tempted, he will also provide a way out so that you can endure it" (1 Corinthians 10.13 NIV).

The world is full of temptations, especially in the USA where we are abundantly blessed with food, entertainment, resources, etc. Whenever we are faced with a choice to consume something, we must ask God: "God, is this for me?" We would rid ourselves of jealous, covetousness and gluttonous appetites if we asked that simple question. God is good. He's not trying to withhold blessings from us. He has exactly what we need each day. We don't need to desire something that's not for us because we are already blessed with every good thing (James 1.17).

**Weight Loss Verse 4: We are God's Handiwork.**

"For we are God's handiwork, created in Christ Jesus to do good works, which God prepared in advance for us to do" (Ephesians 2.10 NIV).

We are God's amazing works of art. No matter your body type, you are beautiful in His eyes. Before we can even take one step on our weight loss journey, we must thank God for the way He has created us. With all the social media out there, we can get trapped in "I wish I had this" or "I wish I looked like that." I'm writing a body image book series for children about loving exactly how we were made, entitled the *Butterfly Princess Books*. In this parable story, Laia must come to grips with her body differences and learn to embrace how she was created. Before we can lose weight, we must embrace who God created us to be.

**Weight Loss Verse 5: We Will Rejoice and be Glad.**

> "This is the day the Lord has made; We will rejoice and be glad in it" (Psalm 118.24 NKJV).

There is so much beauty all around us. If we fully take a look at the breathtaking world God has created and the blessings He has surrounded us with, there won't be room for the constant desire for more. Overeating is a way to fill our lives with good things, and it can become a spiral effect of constantly wanting more. However, if we look and literally "count our blessings," we will see how very much blessed we are. Before we take that next bite or open that new package, let us count a few of our blessings, and we may very well find that the desire for more has left us. When we rejoice and fill our hearts with gladness, eating less or eating differently won't seem as much of an impossibility.

**Weight Loss Verse 6: We Have the Holy Spirit to Help Us.**

> "But when the Father sends the Advocate as my representative—that is, the Holy Spirit—he will teach you everything and will remind you of everything I have told you" (John 14.26 NLT).

Jesus died on the Cross, so we could have God's Spirit, the Holy Spirit, helping us every moment of each day. Jesus died, redeeming us by His grace, so God's Spirit could enter a broken world. Not only can we look forward to being with God in heaven for eternity, but we can also look forward to His presence right here with us on earth. We have the

Comforter in us. We have Jesus interceding for us (Romans 8.34). Jesus has overcome the world on our behalf (John 16.33). And we have the victory in Christ (1 Corinthians 15.57). We can cultivate our intimacy with the Lord, as we rely on Him daily for comfort and strength.

**Weight Loss Verse 7: Fasting is Powerful.**

> "So we fasted and petitioned our God about this, and he answered our prayer" (Ezra 8.23 NIV).

Fasting is a powerful force for God to move in our hearts and circumstances. One fast that will help us with our weight loss journey is intermittent fasting. A simple way to intermittent fast is to skip a different meal each day. If you skip breakfast on Monday, then skip lunch on Tuesday. And if you skip lunch on Tuesday, skip dinner on Wednesday and so forth. Skip one meal a day while not overeating on the other two meals but take the weekends off to eat your normal 3 meals a day. This will not only reap the spiritual benefits of fasting, but it will also give you that calorie deficit your body needs to lose weight. Plus, it will keep your metabolism running strong because it won't be able to get comfortable in a predictable eating routine.

**Weight Loss Verse 8: Don't Try to Please People.**

> "Work willingly at whatever you do, as though you were working for the Lord rather than for people" (Colossians 3.23 NLT).

Our weight loss journey is not to get the approval of people. When our motivation is to work for the Lord, then the pressure of pleasing people is gone. We are already beautiful and valuable in God's eyes. However, He has a lot He wants us to do in this life, and He wants to do a lot through us. He knows that our weight can limit what we do because 1) our health is impeded and 2) our confidence is impeded. When we work towards losing weight for the purposes of God and not the demands of others, our weight loss journey becomes more of an adventure and less of a chore. Not only are we getting an opportunity to draw closer to God, but we also get better at working with Him toward a common goal.

**Weight Loss Verse 9: Pray and Seek God Daily.**

> "Before daybreak the next morning, Jesus got up and went out to an isolated place to pray" (Mark 1.35 NLT).

Jesus faced temptations, death threats, hurting people, unfaithful family and friends and constant scrutiny from others. He had to pray every day and receive the power and strength of God to accomplish His destiny of being the Light into this world (John 8.12). Anytime we begin a difficult journey, we must have our daily time with God, especially when trying to lose weight. If you want to lose weight and keep it off, seek God and receive His overflowing favor, grace and love. With God on your side, there is nothing out there that can stop you from achieving weight loss (Isaiah 54.17).

**Weight Loss Verse 10: You Are Fearfully and Wonderfully Made.**

"I praise you because I am fearfully and wonderfully made; your works are wonderful, I know that full well" (Psalm 139.14 NIV).

Your body has been fearfully and wonderfully made by the God of the universe. Your body is strong, intricate and adaptable. You can set your mind to having the healthy, fit body you've once had or always longed for. All you need to do is decide that the time is now. Remember, if you need a basic guide to jump start your weight loss journey or you need to refresh your motivation, check out my book, *Fearlessly Fit,* which covers food, fitness and faith for complete and lasting health. This Bible study can be done alone or as a group study with friends or a church group.

# DAY 14

## [7 WAYS TO FIND AND KEEP FAITH]

Faith is the belief in things we can't see in the natural. We are of two worlds: the natural and the supernatural. The supernatural is God's Kingdom. The natural has been given to the stewardship of people (Psalm 115.16). However, God wants earth to align with His supernatural Kingdom (Matthew 6.10). He literally wants heaven on earth and for His unlimited Kingdom to overtake our limited world. Faith is belief in His Kingdom and its infiltration into our earth.

> "Now faith is the substance of things hoped for, the evidence of things not seen" (Hebrews 11.1 NKJV).

**Faith in the Messiah.**

Faith must first start with a relationship with God's Son, the Messiah. We can have no part of the supernatural world in our imperfect state. Perfection is required, but we all fall short (Romans 3.23). We must have righteousness (right standing with God) given to us. That is why Jesus' Finished Work on the Cross is the key. It opens the door to God's Kingdom. We only get into God's Kingdom through Jesus.

> "Jesus said to him, 'I am the way, the truth, and the life. No one comes to the Father except through Me'" (John 14.6).

79

When our faith is not aligned with God's Kingdom, it will falter and fade. However, we can keep our faith in 7 simple ways. The Bible says that the Kingdom of God is within us (Luke 17.21). So at any time, we can usher God's supernatural Kingdom into our lives and situations. Here are 7 simple ways to keep faith. They may seem simple, but they will protect your belief in God and His Kingdom.

**How to Keep Faith?**

The Bible says that faith comes through hearing the Word of God. Our heart needs to be filled with Scripture. God's Words are found in the Bible and in other resources that use the Bible as its main source. We can read and listen to God's Words to maintain our faith, so heaven can penetrate our lives. When we are believing God for a promise, breakthrough, healing and revelation, our expectant faith will open the portal to God's supernatural provision and power in our lives. And we keep our faith by surrounding ourselves with God's Word.

> "So then faith comes by hearing, and hearing by the word of God" (Romans 10.17 NKJV).

**Wake Up to the Word to Keep Faith.**

Every morning, I know the devil will start his attacks on my mind. Therefore, I make sure that I'm ready. I grab my phone and instantly fill my room with faith-boosting insights from God's Word. I play a podcast or video of a preacher, prophet, teacher, etc. who I enjoy.

**Listen to Christian Music in the Car to Keep Faith.**

Listening to Christian music may seem difficult at first. You may not know any of the songs or artists. But it won't take long before you'll be singing to the encouraging lyrics. Try to find a Christian station that mixes music with inspirational DJs. You'll be amazed at how God will boost your faith through the music.

**Have Your Bathroom Quiet Times to Keep Faith.**

This does sound weird talking to God in the bathroom. Let's be honest. These short minutes may be the only time you're alone all day. Nevertheless, people use the restroom 6-8 times a day, and those minutes will add up. Pray for others. Pray for your situation. Tell God that you love Him. This can be your constant interaction with God throughout the day to boost your faith.

**Keep Devotional Books Handy to Keep Faith.**

Powerful Christian leaders read and write devotionals. These are short, powerful insights that will keep your faith. You can carry a devotional in your purse, backpack or briefcase. Gleaning from other people will remind you that you're not alone. Additionally, their wisdom may be exactly what you need for that day.

**Go to the Bible App before Social Media to Keep Faith.**

Before you touch the Facebook or Instagram app on your phone, go to your Bible App. YouVersion has the entire Bible and tons of free devotionals at your fingertips. Plus, it's all free with no advertisements. Before you get lost in social media, read a few verses or start a new devotional. Reading devotionals will definitely safeguard your faith.

**Pray at the Moment to Keep Faith.**

God will bring people on your path every day. And these people may share their hurts and pains with you. Instead of saying you'll pray for them, just pray for them right there. It may be uncomfortable at first, but just ask, "Can I pray for you now?" Grab their hand, bow your head and pray for their situation in Jesus' name. Just make the prayer simple. This supernatural interaction with others will help keep your faith strong!

**Do Something Sweet and Secret to Keep Faith.**

Listen to the Holy Spirit. He wants to use you to bless others. Try to find at least one person a day that you can bless in secret. Helping others will not only boost your faith, but it will make you feel great. Donate clothes. Offer encouraging words to a stranger. Babysit for a friend. Send a gift to a ministry leader. Pray for a stranger on the street. Do something tangible for someone each day. When you give, you will receive (Luke 6.38).

# DAY 15

# [5 TRUTHS TO SPEAK OVER YOUR KIDS]

Every morning, I declare these 5 biblical truths over my kids before they leave the house. The Bible has so much power, but we must activate it. When our kids experience our activation of God's Word, they will learn to activate it for themselves. All God's promises in the Bible are potentially ours. We simply need to find them, believe them, declare them and receive them.

**Truth 1: You are the Righteousness of God in Jesus Christ.**

Your kids are beautiful and amazing in God's eyes. If they have accepted Jesus as their Lord and Savior, God sees them through the Blood of Jesus Christ. They have right-standing with God because of Jesus' Finished Work on the Cross. No matter their mistakes and mess-ups, they never lose their righteous position in Christ. If they haven't accepted Jesus yet, you can tell them about the amazing love that God has for them, and He sent His Son to die for them and bring them back into relationship with God.

> "For He made Him who knew no sin to be sin for us, that we might become the righteousness of God in Him" (2 Corinthians 5.21 NKJV).

**Truth 2: You are the Head, not the Tail.**

83

The Bible says that your kids have the victory. No matter their popularity, grades, wardrobe or looks, they rise to the top with God. God sees them as mighty and worthy warriors. God places infinite value on them.

> "And the Lord will make you the head and not the tail; you shall be above only, and not be beneath, if you heed the commandments of the Lord your God, which I command you today, and are careful to observe them" (Deuteronomy 28.13 NKJV).

**Truth 3: You have the Victory in Jesus Christ.**

No matter the odds against them, your kids have the victory. God uses ALL things (even temporary failures) for His ultimate good and Kingdom plan (Romans 8.28). They don't have to worry! As they are following Jesus, they will win at life.

> "But thanks be to God, who gives us the victory through our Lord Jesus Christ" (1 Corinthians 15.57 NKJV).

**Truth 4: You walk in God's Supernatural Authority.**

Because of the Work of Jesus on the Cross, your kids have God's Spirit inside of them. Their sins are forgiven, so the authority of the Holy Spirit is theirs. They have supernatural authority over their enemies in Jesus' powerful name.

> "Behold, I give you the authority to trample on serpents and scorpions, and over all the power of the enemy, and nothing shall by any means hurt you" (Luke 10.19 NKJV).

**Truth 5: You are loved by Your Creator God.**

Most of the problems of our kids today would disappear if they knew just how much they are loved. Beloved people don't fall for the petty traps of the enemy. Beloved people don't accept harmful lifestyle choices. They are too loved to bother with anything less than God's best.

> "For God so loved the world that He gave His only begotten Son, that whoever believes in Him should not perish but have everlasting life" (John 3.16 NKJV).

# DAY 16

## [5 VERSES TO BOOST YOUR FAITH]

Remember as a little kid during the summer, you stood on the diving board staring down at the translucent water. You could see all the way down to the bottom of the 8-foot pool, and your young mind said, "This isn't possible. If you jump, you will fall and hurt yourself." However, your family and friends coaxed in reassuring voices, "It's okay! Just jump!"

And as you hovered over the water, your mind tried to reason. However, there is no reasoning when it comes to jumping into water. You have to trust that it will catch you— though, in the natural, it seems impossible. The more you wait, the more you hesitate and the greater chance you will turn away and walk slowly back to the ladder where it is safe.

The same is true for faith. God calls you to do something, to go somewhere – to make a choice to follow His promptings. And if you reason, you will talk yourself out of obeying. In this moment, reasoning is the killer of faith. Not to say that God isn't a God of order, but His order is greater than the order of the world's systems. His plan usurps even the most basic principles of our reality on earth. If He calls, He will provide.

Instead of trying to reason with human understanding, we can claim these five promises from God in His Word. They will fuel your faith, so you can finally take the leap into the great unknown, trusting that the Living Water of God's provision will catch us. And once we dive in, we will jump again with greater confidence. When we experience God "Catching" us in our leap of faith, we will live out a lifestyle of trusting, obeying and jumping when He leads.

The following are five promises to help you when your faith is wavering. Instead of reasoning, repeat them over and over again until they become absorbed into your mind, heart and, finally, your actions. Trust that the Living Water will catch you when you take a leap of faith.

**Verse 1 to Boost Your Faith.**

> "'For my thoughts are not your thoughts, neither are your ways my ways,' declares the Lord. 'As the heavens are higher than the earth, so are my ways higher than your ways and my thoughts than your thoughts'" (Isaiah 55.8-9 NIV).

God's thoughts and ways are many times beyond our understanding. We can align our thoughts with His as much as possible, but eventually a choice of faith will have to be made. This choice to trust God despite what our earthly eyes can discern proves that we believe God more than we believe our circumstances.

**Verse 2 to Boost Your Faith.**

> "Now faith is confidence in what we hope for and assurance about what we do not see" (Hebrews 11.1 NIV).

Faith is a normal part of living for God. If there isn't something we are hoping and trusting for that seems impossible in the natural, we are not truly walking in the fullness of our destiny. Faith pleases God (Hebrews 11.6). And those who hope in God will not be put to shame (Psalm 25.3).

**Verse 3 to Boost Your Faith.**

> "And we know that in all things God works for the good of those who love him, who have been called according to his purpose" (Romans 8.28 NIV).

We can trust that all our choices made by faith in accordance with God's will always work out to our good and to the good of others. It may only take a few days; however, it may take decades for our faith steps to lead into the unveiling of God's glorious plan. But, eventually, our steps of faith will reap a harvest that not only we can enjoy, but we can share with the people around us and for generations to come.

**Verse 4 to Boost Your Faith.**

> "I can do all this through him who gives me strength" (Philippians 4.13 NIV).

"All things" is a very strong, definitive promise. If God has called us, we can trust that He will give us the innovative strength to do it. In fact, we can walk in a confident boldness, knowing that God's grace is supplying everything we lack (Hebrews 4.16). We don't have to hesitate in our faith because God's provision is always pouring out into us and our situations.

**Verse 5 to Boost Your Faith.**

> "For the wisdom of this world is foolishness to God. As the Scriptures say, 'He traps the wise in the snare of their own cleverness'" (1 Corinthians 3.19 NLT).

If we try to analyze our steps of faith by the wisdom of the world, we will talk ourselves out of obeying. The wisdom of this world is mere foolishness to the imaginative supremacy of a God Who can achieve all things, no matter how impossible they seem. He has the resources of heaven and earth at His disposal, and what is impossible for us is totally possible for Him (Luke 18.27).

**Diving into Your Destiny.**

So the next time you find yourself on the diving board of indecision, and you hear the voice of your Heavenly Father calling you to take a leap of faith, don't hesitate. Jump into the watery depths of His will, knowing that He loves you more than you can comprehend, and He will catch you as you dive into your destiny.

> "Then Christ will make his home in your hearts as you trust in him. Your roots will grow down into God's love and keep you strong. And may you have the power to understand, as all God's people should, how wide, how long, how high, and how deep his love is" (Ephesians 3.17-18 NLT).

# DAY 17

## [5 COUNTERFEITS OF JESUS]

As the expression goes, there may be "more than one way to skin a cat," but there is only One way to be in the presence of God in heaven. This One way is Jesus. In our human-centered understanding, we try to make up other avenues to get to heaven. Also, the enemy of our souls manufactures lie after lie, desperate to keep us distracted from the Truth. But God made it clear by prophecy in the Old Testament and reality in the New Testament. He was sending a Messiah, a Christ, a Savior, a Hero, a Son to save the world. Jesus is the only way to be with God in heaven.

> "I am the way and the truth and the life. No one comes to the Father except through me" (John 14.6 NIV).

**Counterfeit Number 1: "You can't know for sure."**

To me, this is the worst counterfeit of them all. That a Creator would pour out His creativity, energy and love into a creation and not give them a for sure way to connect with Him. A loving parent would never leave their children stranded. We are not in the dark. The Bible makes the truth plain and clear. Jesus is our portal from this life to the presence of God. All we have to do is see our need for a Mediator and use our words backed by belief to claim Jesus as our Lord and Savior.

"If you declare with your mouth, 'Jesus is Lord,' and believe in your heart that God raised him from the dead, you will be saved. For it is with your heart that you believe and are justified, and it is with your mouth that you profess your faith and are saved" (Romans 10.9-10 NIV).

## Counterfeit Number 2: "You have to be good enough."

Here is the thing: no matter how good we are, we will never be good enough to be in the presence of a holy God without a mediator. We believe this counterfeit when we are either ignorant or in denial about how awesome and perfect our God is. God knew we would fall short of His holy standard, which is why He sent His Son to make atonement for our sins. Jesus gave us His holiness, and He took our sins. It is only through Jesus we will ever be good enough because we receive His perfection by grace.

"For all have sinned and fall short of the glory of God, and all are justified freely by his grace through the redemption that came by Christ Jesus" (Romans 3.23-24 NIV).

## Counterfeit Number 3: "You get a do-over."

Reincarnation suggests that if we aren't good enough in our current life, we will get another life to try again. This is false in two ways. First, it relies on counterfeit number 2 that we can be good enough, which we can't. Second, believing in reincarnation takes more faith than believing in Jesus because there is no biblical backing. In Jesus, we are "born again" meaning that our spirits are "birthed" into a relationship with a holy God. This relationship continues

91

after our bodies die and we enter heaven. We are physically born through our mother and spiritually born through our Savior. Our flesh and spirit are tethered into a one-of-a-kind, unique masterpiece. God doesn't discard our life for another because this life He is giving us now is precious and valuable.

> "For we are God's handiwork, created in Christ Jesus to do good works, which God prepared in advance for us to do" (Ephesians 2.10 NIV).

**Counterfeit Number 4: "There are many ways."**

Jesus is God in the flesh Who came down to earth to break His body and pour out His Blood. The Blood of Jesus Christ is the Living Water of God mixed with the earth to redeem all of creation from sin. Through the Blood of Jesus Christ, we can now have a relationship with a holy God because we have been made right. That relationship continues into eternity. Nothing or no one can accomplish what Jesus has accomplished. All of creation pivots on His Sacrifice on the Cross and His Redeeming Blood. To accept Jesus is to walk in God's presence. To reject Jesus is to walk in the absence of God's presence. Nothing other than the Blood of Jesus can birth us into the presence of God. Nothing is that powerful.

> "How much more, then, will the blood of Christ, who through the eternal Spirit offered himself unblemished to God, cleanse our consciences from acts that lead to death, so that we may serve the living God!" (Hebrews 9.14 NIV).

**Counterfeit Number 5: "You don't matter."**

The Bible says that Jesus died for each single one of us. He loves you. No matter how you were raised, what sins you have committed or how you see yourself, God adores you. You are His child. He longs to have a relationship with you, which is why He sent Jesus to die in order to redeem your sins. If you would like to have a relationship with God, all you have to do is accept Jesus as your Lord and Savior. Say these words:

*"Dear Jesus, I know that I'm a sinner. I fall short of God's holy standard. Yet, I still want to be part of His royal family. I want to live with God in heaven for eternity. I ask for You, Jesus, to come into my heart. Forgive me of my sins. And be my Lord and Savior. Thank You for loving and saving me. I pray this in Jesus' name, amen."*

"And he died for all, that those who live should no longer live for themselves but for him who died for them and was raised again" (2 Corinthians 5.15 NIV).

# DAY 18

# [4 NATURAL WAYS TO CREATE PEACE IN YOUR HOME]

"I love coming into your home! It's so peaceful."

I hear these words all the time. Family and friends know that I desire peace in my home, especially since the world can be hectic, chaotic and rushed. My home is a safe haven of sorts, a heaven on earth while we live here. Creating an atmosphere for Jesus to extend His peace takes strategy and imagination. I see every day, every moment, like a scene in a chapter of our lives. And any good writer knows that you can, with the words and actions you choose, create a scene to be powerful and purposeful. I simply create space for Jesus' peace to flood my home.

Peace has power and purpose. It frees us up to hear from the Lord and receive love and show love to Him. It allows the people within our home to experience God's kindness and clarity. When we come into an atmosphere of peace, we can let go of the inner struggle, heartache and confusion we have been holding onto. When those negative emotions are released into an atmosphere of peace, they evaporate in the warmth of God's love and compassion for us. As people come into our home, we can literally offer peace to their spirits. This offering is priceless.

> "Peace I leave with you; my peace I give you. I do not give to you as the world gives. Do not let your hearts be troubled and do not be afraid" (John 14.27 NIV).

**4 Natural Ways to Create Peace.**

Because humans are both spirit and flesh, there are natural and supernatural ways to promote peace in the home. The natural ways put our body at ease. The supernatural ways put our spirit at ease. Both are important, especially if we are offering peace to the young and hurting. Learning to have peace in the midst of the storm takes experience and maturity, so for now we will create a peace that is both tangible and experiential.

> "And let the peace that comes from Christ rule in your hearts. For as members of one body you are called to live in peace. And always be thankful" (Colossians 3.15 NLT).

**Natural Way 1: An Organized Home.**

I know this may sound simple and kind of old fashion, but the clutter of our home will negatively affect those within it. This doesn't mean that our home should be show-worthy at any moment but picking up and putting things where they belong will promote peace. Everything has its place. Forming a habit of putting things back where they belong will save time and energy. Teaching our kids to pick up after themselves shows good stewardship of what they've been blessed with. And when people come into our homes, they will feel like they've entered a place of stability and peacefulness.

> "But be sure that everything is done properly and in order" (1 Corinthians 14.40 NLT).

**Natural Way 2: A Nice Smelling Home.**

According to research, our sense of smell is closely linked to memories, and it is a highly emotional sense. As we create peaceful scenes in our home, the smell of our home will enrich the moment, creating lasting memories in the minds and hearts of others. Using candles, wick-less candles, plug-ins, diffusers and sprays will create beautiful, emotionally rooted, moments of peace that will last a lifetime. We can even get creative, using certain scents for certain moments of time to really package the atmosphere with temporal peace that can touch the supernatural.

> "I jumped up to open the door for my love, and my hands dripped with perfume. My fingers dripped with lovely myrrh as I pulled back the bolt" (Song of Solomon 5.5 NLT).

**Natural Way 3: A Sustenance Home.**

I know that a lot of people do not cook, but that shouldn't stop us from offering a beverage and/or snack to our guests. When I have people over, I do a hybrid of some home cooked items with some packaged items. The easiest offering is fruit with cheese and crackers. Super simple and people enjoy the variety. There once was a time when breaking bread together was the catalyst for friendships and special moments. Keeping food ready for visitors is a sure way to bless them. Thirst and hunger satisfied allows peace to come to the forefront.

> "And the King will say, 'I tell you the truth, when you did it to one of the least of these my brothers and sisters, you were doing it to me!'" (Matthew 25.40 NLT).

**Natural Way 4: A Musical Home.**

I have an Amazon Echo that I play Christian music on, but any form of producing music will do. According to research, music is a phenomenon that is deeply rooted into our minds. Calming and inspiring music can alleviate stress, anxiety and pain. I will play worship music, soaking music and/or instrumental music depending on the mood I want to create. In the evenings when I cook dinner, I enjoy listening to smooth jazz. I try to keep music always filling the atmosphere of my home. Christian music that speaks words of biblical truth are awesome at filling my home with the aroma of God's goodness.

> "And whenever the tormenting spirit from God troubled Saul, David would play the harp. Then Saul would feel better, and the tormenting spirit would go away"(1 Samuel 16.23 NLT).

# DAY 19

## [8 TRICKS TO ADD A WORKOUT TO YOUR DAY]

**Making Exercise a Priority.**

Much of the western world has cultivated a sedentary lifestyle. Because of technology much of our work is done at the computer, and much of our entertainment is done in front of a screen. Advancements in technology give us both benefits and hindrances, and we must make changes to compensate for both. We have been quick to accept the benefits of technology, but we've had trouble adjusting to the hindrances, one of which is a lack of exercise.

We don't have to milk a cow. We don't have to walk to the store. We don't have to till our own ground. Our daily exercise has been lost, which is why we have to create our own. Our bodies and souls were created to enjoy the vigor of exercise. Without it, we lack energy, stamina and mental sharpness.

We fill our schedules with busyness, and we think we don't have time to work out. However, our priorities will always dictate their presence in our day. What we deem most important will inevitably make its way into our daily activities. Therefore, we need to understand the overarching importance of exercise to our health and quality of life, so we can make it a priority.

If we don't feel good, we can't fully embrace others and our destiny. To be sure, God will give us grace when we are sick, and that sickness is out of our control. However, there are repercussions to living a sedentary lifestyle that we are fully capable of avoiding if we were to simply add exercise to our schedule.

The following are 8 tricks to add 30 minutes of exercise into a busy schedule. Make exercise a priority, and I promise you'll find a way to fit it into your day.

### Trick 1 to Fit in a 30-Minute Workout: Wake up 30 minutes Early.

I know this one seems basic, but it is one of the easiest ways to get your exercise done and feel good the rest of the day. Fasted exercise (working out before breakfast) can kickstart your metabolism and create a hunger for breakfast. Set your morning alarm 35 minutes earlier. This will give you five minutes to get ready and thirty minutes to work out. Then you can jump into the shower like usual and get ready for your day. However, now you will feel energized and awake. Plus, you will have an important priority checked off your to-do list, which will boost your confidence the rest of the day. Once you make waking up 35 minutes earlier as a priority, your body and mind will easily adapt to this healthy habit.

### Trick 2 to Fit in a 30-Minute Workout: Combine Your Quiet Time with your Workout.

Many people aim to pray and read their Bible 30 minutes a day. Why not combine your workout with your prayer time? You can go for a walk and listen to the Bible on a Bible App or on Audible. Then when you've read (listened) to about 10-15 minutes of Scripture, you can switch to worship music and pray for your needs and for the needs of others. You can also worship the Father and let Him know how thankful you are for all His blessings. You will be surprised at how being thankful and recognizing all God's goodness will uplift your spirit.

**Trick 3 to Fit in a 30-Minute Workout: Combine Your Entertainment with your Workout.**

This one takes a little training, but soon you'll be able to work out while allowing your mind to be entertained by a show, book, video, Podcast, etc. One of my favorite exercises while watching a show is to take a basic aerobic, stackable step or bench and small hand weights. Then, I step up and down on the bench doing bicep curls with my hand weights for a 30-minute show or longer. But be careful! One time I watched an entire 2-hour movie while stepping, and my calves were sore for a week. You can listen to an audiobook while riding a stationary bike. You can watch a show while walking/jogging on a treadmill. The possibilities are endless.

**Trick 4 to Fit in a 30-Minute Workout: Pack Your Lunch and Walk the Stairs.**

If you work at an office, instead of going out to lunch (which usually has more calories and costs more money) bring a packed lunch instead. This will not only save you money but time. If your office building has stairs, grab your headphones and walk the stairs going up and down for thirty minutes while listening to upbeat music. Then you can cool down at your desk while eating your healthy lunch.

If you don't have stairs, then you can use a simple workout app that offers an exercise program using your own body weight. Or you can take a nice walk outside for thirty minutes. Whatever you decide, just get your body moving during lunch.

**Trick 5 to Fit in a 30-Minute Workout: Find a New Hobby that Keeps You Active.**

There are so many fun things to do that don't include sitting in front of a screen. Why not take up a new hobby or revisit an old hobby? You can go golfing, swimming, salsa dancing, fishing, cycling, kayaking – there are so many exciting activities that get the heart rate going. If you are married, you can learn a new hobby with your spouse. Not only will you get exercise, but you will be adding quality time to your marriage. Or grab some friends and/or siblings and plan a weekly activity together.

**Trick 6 to Fit in a 30-Minute Workout: Don't Just Sit There and Wait. Get Moving.**

If you are a parent, you know that your kids have so many activities. From piano lessons to ballet lessons to football practice and band practice, your kids stay busy and keep you busy waiting. Instead of just sitting in the lobby waiting for your kid to finish his/her 30-minute lesson, why not use that time to get moving? When my daughter took ballet, I would drop her off and take a thirty-minute jog. When my son had football practice, I would walk around the track. When my other son had piano lessons at the mall, I would walk the mall. There is no need to just sit there looking through social media on your phone. Keep a good pair of running shoes in your car, so whenever you must wait, you can move instead.

**Trick 7 to Fit in a 30-Minute Workout: Make the Park your Personal Gym.**

When my kids were very young, I used to take them to the park. While they were running around getting their exercise, I would get in a quick workout, as well. I used all the different elements of the playground as my personal gym. The curb became my box for box jumps. The picnic table was used for triceps dips. The monkey bars allowed me to do pull-ups or hanging pull-ups (holding a pull-up position for 30 seconds). I would do lunges down the field. Push-ups on the basketball court. I would intermix some basic training exercises—jumping jacks, sit-ups and sprints – while keeping a watchful eye on my kids. After 30 minutes of exercise, I too was ready for my afternoon nap.

**Trick 8 to Fit in a 30-Minute Workout: Do your Workout in Increments.**

If all else fails, and you just can't get a full 30-minutes, you can break your workout into increments. For example, when you go to the grocery store, park at the end of the lot and take a 3 to 5-minute walk to the store. If you must take an elevator, take the stairs instead. If you must get the mail, walk to the mailbox if it is farther away. If you're at the airport, skip the moving walkway and walk to your gate. Make every effort to get in 6 to 10 increments of exercise (3-5 minutes) a day, and you will hit your 30-minute mark.

If you want to lose weight and gain muscle, check out my at-home exercise book, *Fearlessly Fit at Home.* This exercise program incorporates cardio calisthenics with dumbbell weightlifting for a full body, fat burning workout. However, always consult your physician before starting a new exercise program.

# DAY 20

# [11 PRACTICES OF MY QUIET TIME]

I have found that as I pray daily, I am more prepared when crisis hits. I also have a greater sense of well-being after I've allowed God's goodness to pour over me. I don't have to wait until a problem occurs to enjoy time with God. My relationship with Him is deepened, and I'm filled with His goodness each new day as I rest in His presence. I have experienced times of deep discouragement, which opened me up to intense spiritual attack in my weakened state. If we don't seek God daily, the heavy cloak of disappointment, hopelessness and fear will cause us to be too weak to resist the enemy's schemes (James 4.7). It is so much better to turn to God during daily prayer and Bible reading, so we are prepared for every high and low of life. We can appreciate the good times more, and the bad times won't expose us to the enemy's lies when we have a habit of spending time with God.

Although I pray constantly during the day, I do have a special time with God that is more intentional. Here is what I do. You can use my time with the Lord as a blueprint to kickstart your prayer time. The more you learn in Christ, the more tools you will have in your prayer-time arsenal to live a victorious life. And soon enough, you'll be able to create a quiet time that is tailored to your needs and to the season in which you find yourself.

**First, Create a Prayer Nook.**

I have a place in my master bedroom right under the windows that I use as my prayer nook. I used to pray in my closet, but I wanted a place where my kids could go when they weren't feeling well–physically and emotionally. I have a floor divider that separates my prayer nook from the rest of my bedroom. I have pillows, blankets, a candle, a speaker for "soaking" music, my Bible, a journal, anointing oils and Eucharist elements in that space. My hope is that the area becomes so saturated with God's presence that it permeates the rest of the house. I also want my anointing oils to become saturated, so I can anoint people, homes and other items that need a blessing (Mark 6.13 & 1 John 2.27). Plus, I try to do communion every day as I receive the bread of Christ (His provision) and the Blood of Christ (His forgiveness and cleansing) each day (1 Corinthians 11.26).

**Second, Release the Isaiah Spirits.**

Every promise in the Bible is ours, but we must learn to identify and claim them. There are 7 spirits found in Isaiah 11.2 (NASB). 1) The Spirit of the LORD 2) The Spirit of wisdom 3) The Spirit of understanding 4) The Spirit of counsel 5) The Spirit of strength 6) The Spirit of knowledge 7) The Spirit of the fear of the LORD. I begin my time with the Lord releasing these spirits into my life. I want to make sure my time with the Lord is profoundly effective. I've spent years whining to God and being counterproductive during my prayer time. Now I'm very intentional to start my time on a more powerful, productive setting.

**Third, Loose the Fruits of the Spirit**.

Because I have God's Spirit in me, I have access to His amazing fruits every moment. I want to remind myself of these fruits and activate my faith to claim them. They are found in Galatians 5.22-23 (NLT). They include Love, Joy, Peace, Patience, Kindness, Goodness, Faithfulness, Gentleness and Self-Control. I want each one, but some days I'm in dire need of a specific one. For example, if I'm feeling discouraged, I may aggressively claim Joy. Or if I feel stressed out, I claim Peace. And if I feel like I've gotten too glutenous with food, entertainment, leisure, etc., I claim Self-Control. These fruits are mine by adoption into God's family through Jesus Christ, and I have every right to claim their goodness and provision in my life (John 1.12).

**Fourth, Put on the Armor.**

Next, I put on the Armor of God. This part of my prayer time is very important to me. I want my heart, mind and actions to be protected. I also want the ability to take ground that the enemy has sought to control. I know that my fight is not just against flesh and blood; it is supernatural, and I need to be prepared (Ephesians 6:12 NLT). First, I put on the Belt of Truth. I want every lie of the enemy evident and disposed of. I want to see myself according to my identity in Christ.

Second, I put on the Breastplate of Righteousness. This armor protects my heart's feelings and emotions from the enemy's schemes. Third, my feet are protected with the Gospel Shoes of Peace. This means that wherever I go and whatever happens, I always have the Peace of Jesus Christ with me (John 14.27). I don't have to be frantic or dismayed. Fourth, I put on my Helmet of Salvation. My mind's thoughts and imaginings are protected from the enemy's lies because I renew my mind each day in Christ. I let go of things that happened in the past (which Jesus has already redeemed) and move forward with a clean slate. Fifth, I hold up my Shield of Faith. The fiery darts of the enemy don't have to make it to my body armor because I have faith that God will always turn everything to my good (Romans 8.28). The arrows of accusation will transform into words of blessings. Finally, I wield my Sword of the Spirit, which is the Holy Spirit's presence in my life and God's Holy Word, the Bible. When I listen to God's Words via His Spirit and the Bible, I can take an offensive stance and take ground for God's Kingdom.

**Fifth, Pray the Priestly Prayer.**

Then, I pray the Priestly Prayer of Blessing over my family and me. I would suggest reading Warren Marcus's book, *Priestly Prayer of Blessing*. You will see my top-rated review on the book's Amazon page. Marcus explains that this prayer is a blessing that offers us a personal God Who wants His goodness to flow in our lives. Below is the prayer.

> "The Lord bless you, and keep you [protect you, sustain you, and guard you]; The Lord make His face shine upon you [with favor], And be gracious to you [surrounding you with lovingkindness]; The Lord lift up His countenance (face) upon you [with divine approval], And give you peace [a tranquil heart and life]" (Numbers 6.24-26 AMP).

**Sixth, Tuck My Spirit.**

After I have declared all of the promises and saturated my mind, heart and atmosphere with God's presence, I tuck my body and soul into my spirit. Just like God, we are made up of three parts. God is God the Father (Creator), Jesus the Son (Savior) and Holy Spirit the Helper (Counselor). We too are made up of three parts: We are Soul, Body and, through Jesus Christ, we are also Spirit. Our spirits are dead and separated from God because of sin; but through Jesus' Sacrifice on the Cross, we have been given His righteousness in exchange for our sin and now our spirit comes alive and is united with God. It is our spirit that is sinless and resting in God's presence always. It is in the spirit where we have power, strength, comfort, peace, joy, love and power.

I want to submit my body and my soul, which is made up of my mind (thoughts and imaginings), my heart (feelings and emotions) and my will (my decisions and habits) to my spirit. I want to be spirit driven, not body or soul driven. My body and soul are important, but they only function well when they are both submitted to my spirit. Once I've tucked my body and soul into my spirit, I now confess that my spirit is tucked into Christ (Philippians 3.9) and Christ is at the right-hand side of God (Colossians 3.1). Therefore, all three parts of me (body, soul and spirit) are at the right-hand side of God in the Courts of Heaven.

**Seventh, Declare My Innocence.**

Once I find myself in the courts of heaven in Christ, I now declare my innocence before all of heaven and earth. The enemy is always accusing us (Revelation 21.10). He wants to steal our destiny, kill our influence and destroy our lives (John 10.10). We must never side with the enemy's accusations towards us. Even in little things, we must guard our hearts above all else (Proverbs 4.23). I use my words to declare my innocence and righteousness in Christ (Romans 3.22) and I rebuke every accusation, lie and sickness from the enemy. I wield my shield of faith to block every fiery dart that the devil throws at me. I ask for the Living Water of God to flush my mind of any false imaginings or thoughts (John 7.38) and to wash away all negative emotions and feelings. I declare that the curses of the enemy are transformed instantly into blessings through the resurrection power of Jesus Christ (Philippians 3.10-11). I stop all useless dialogue with the enemy. The devil wants to keep us so distracted defending ourselves that we stop walking in our destiny. Hence, I declare that I am innocent through Christ and the case is closed forever!

**Eighth, Prayer, Petition and Thanksgiving**.

Now that I'm reminded of my innocence, I pray, petition and thank God (Philippians 4.6). I thank Him for every blessing that I have in my life. I remind myself of all that God has done for me and declare that He is always working for my good (Jeremiah 29.11). God can resurrect every evil situation into a blessing (Isaiah 61.3). If I am facing something difficult, I profess my belief that God will transform it into something wonderful. After thanking and praising God, I give Him my prayer requests. I pray specific prayers for my family and friends. I don't whine about the problems; rather, I declare the solutions by faith. I also pray back every promise that God has given me, believing that those promises are already accomplished in Jesus' name.

**Ninth, Bible Reading.**

Now I open my Bible and fill my mind, heart and life with the living presence of God's active Word (Hebrews 4.12). The Bible is my Sword, helping me to apply God's truth to my life. The truth of God sets me free from the deceit of the devil and this world, so I want to know as much of this truth as possible (John 8.32). I read God's Word and allow the Holy Spirit to apply its truth to my life. No matter what, I know that reading God's Word is pouring His power, goodness and truth into my being, establishing my steps and preparing my way. I also read and/or listen to other anointed Christian resources. It never fails that God will send me a book, podcast or sermon that speaks to me exactly what I need. Remember, if you are looking for a daily devotional, my book, *Slay the Day*, has 365 short, powerful devotionals that will bless you.

**Tenth, Listen to the Holy Spirit.**

Then, I listen for the Holy Spirit's words. Our Sword is both the written Word and the audible voice of God. God speaks to me daily through moments, through others and through my being still and listening. Many times, God will give me names of people or circumstances in our world to pray for. God will also tell me how He sees me by reminding me of His promises from the Bible. I am His precious daughter (2 Corinthians 6.18). I have an amazing destiny (Romans 8.28-29). I am so loved by God (John 3.16). I am a royal priest (1 Peter 2.9). I sit in the Heavenly Father's presence and soak in all His beautiful words for me. Sometimes, He speaks a lot. Other times, He sits quietly with me. Either way, I communicate with God in voiceless words of power, love, grace, peace and victory.

**Eleventh, Speak in Tongues.**

I also try to speak in tongues while I'm in my prayer time, especially when I'm at a loss for words. The Holy Spirit knows what I need or what to pray when I do not. It may feel weird at first praying in a language you do not know, but we must have faith that our voices are being used to utter the deep things of God.

> "In the same way the Spirit [comes to us and] helps us in our weakness. We do not know what prayer to offer or how to offer it as we should, but the Spirit Himself [knows our need and at the right time] intercedes on our behalf with sighs and groanings too deep for words" (Romans 8.26 AMP).

Sometimes my prayer time lasts only 15 minutes. Other times, my prayer time lasts hours. Either way, I go through this devotional routine with God, and it strengthens and empowers me to live victoriously every day. And when I get hit with something painful or difficult, I won't be wearing a heavy garment of discouragement because I will have allowed God to renew me each day. Having this time with God is like spending time with your best friend Who can supernaturally provide you with everything you need to live abundantly each day (John 10.9-10). If you want to live an abundant life that is filled with meaning and purpose, spend time with God every day. Your life will be transformed.

# DAY 21

# [5 WAYS WE CAN WAIT ON GOD]

"But Lord, be merciful to us, for we have waited for you [REST]. Be our strong arm each day [RELY] and our salvation in times of trouble [RECEIVE]" (Isaiah 33.2 NLT).

**How we can Rest, Rely and Receive.**

Many of us have it all backward. We pray to Receive from God before we've learned to Rest and Rely on Him daily. When we find ourselves in a jam, we cry out to be rescued. However, if we would learn to simply seek Him and wait on Him every day, we wouldn't be in the predicament in the first place. Yes, some circumstances are out of our control, but many of those same difficult situations are heightened because we haven't cultivated a lifestyle of resting and relying on God.

God says that He will be our salvation in times of trouble. This is reactive because God is responding to our desperate situation. God also says that He's our strength each day. This is proactive because resting and relying on God will help us avoid and/or stand strong in difficulties.

Taking time each day to spend with God will give us a holy ease. It doesn't mean life will magically become fair and easy, but it does mean that we can go the way Jesus is going. When we stop going our own way (Isaiah 53.6), we can learn how to walk with God each day (Micah 6.8).

**5 Ways We can Wait on God.**

Waiting on God is one of the most difficult things to learn as a Christian. We want to go our own way and fight our own battles. We struggle with trusting God and carry disbelief that God is faithful. Yet, this is the time to completely depend on what the Bible says and not our own emotions. True submission to God is saying, "You know better than I do. I commit my will and life to You daily." How many times have we looked back on our decisions and choices and regretted them? As we continually seek God first, we can trust that no matter what lies ahead, we have the ultimate victory in Christ.

> "I have told you all this so that you may have peace in me. Here on earth you will have many trials and sorrows. But take heart, because I have overcome the world" (John 16.33 NLT).

Here are 5 ways we can wait on God, so we can rely on His strength every day. He wants to be our daily strong arm, not simply our once in a while desperate plea.

**Way 1: God is Concerned.**

People don't wait on those they deem as indifferent. To believe God doesn't care shows a massive ignorance of God and His Word. He cares so much about us that He would send His Beloved Son to die for us, so we could have a relationship with Him. If God cares enough to give His life for us while we were yet sinners, He also cares about the daily decisions and actions we must make and take. We can wait on Him, knowing that He will guide us along His best path.

113

"But God showed his great love for us by sending Christ to die for us while we were still sinners" (Romans 5.8 NLT).

## Way 2: God Knows More.

To not wait on God tells Him that we think we know better than He does. This obviously is not true. Although we don't say it outright, we tell God that we know more than He does with our actions. Once we conclude that God knows much more than we do, we will stop forging ahead without consulting Him. God will let us entangle ourselves in our self-willed choices and actions until we are so trapped that we must seek Him. How much better we would be if we would have come to God first.

"Seek the Kingdom of God above all else, and live righteously, and he will give you everything you need" (Matthew 6.33 NLT).

## Way 3: God has a Plan.

What an amazing truth: God has a plan! God's Kingdom Plan stretches across space and time. We get to play our part, but we need to know what our part is and how to walk in it each day. The enemy wants to distract us, so we completely miss our destiny. Every day the devil plants bombs of distraction just waiting for us to step on them. But God sees all and knows all. When we seek God and wait on Him, we will sidestep all the landmines and walk in our purpose.

"Patient endurance is what you need now, so that you will continue to do God's will. Then you will receive all that he has promised" (Hebrews 10.36 NLT).

## Way 4: God has Provision.

Miracles happen in the wilderness. God will literally have us take steps of obedience that bring us into a place of need and reliance on Him. These God-ordained wilderness walks are part of God's Word and Plan. God will strip us of all our strength, ingenuity and resources to show us that He is our Mighty Provider. He is not bound by the laws of this world, and He can do the supernatural in our natural situation. When we stop begging scraps from the world, God will begin to show Himself as our mighty Source.

> "And this same God who takes care of me will supply all your needs from his glorious riches, which have been given to us in Christ Jesus" (Philippians 4.19 NLT).

## Way 5: God Desires Relationship.

Above all else, God wants to know us and spend time with us because our joy is found in Him. He doesn't need us, but He chooses to have a relationship with us because of His great love. He wants us to seek Him during both good and bad times. The relationship God has with us came at a high price (His Son on the Cross), and He doesn't want us to squander it away with busyness and distraction. He desires to be our Father and Provider in all areas as we learn to Rest and Rely on Him each day and Receive from His goodness in all circumstances.

"You haven't done this before. Ask, using my name, and you will receive, and you will have abundant joy" (John 16.24 NLT).

# DAY 22

# [5 FACTS ON SPRINTS: AN EASY WAY TO LOSE WEIGHT]

**One: How to Make Time for Sprints.**

Finding time to exercise can be difficult with the many responsibilities pulling at us each day. Many times, we think we need a gym membership or an entire hour to get a good workout. But neither is true. All we need are running shoes, 20-25 minutes and a small stretch of land.

Doing sprints is a great substitute for a normal workout or for when there isn't much time. And the best part is that sprints can be done anywhere! It may seem weird at first doing sprints in random places, but the benefits to overall health and fitness are worth it.

Running sprints is a high-intensity workout that does an amazing job of getting the heart rate up and increasing the metabolism – two things that keep us healthy, fit and feeling good. So grab your running shoes and make a run for it.

**Two: Here's How to do Sprints.**

- Keep running shoes in your car or travel bag.
- Find a small stretch of land clear of obstacles (around 50-100 yards).
- Run the distance (about 20-30 seconds), pushing to reach your target heart rate.

- Walk back to the starting point, allowing your heart rate to go back down (around a minute and a half).
- Repeat the sprints 10 to 15 times.
- Stretch when finished while the muscles are loose and warm.

**Three: Here's Where to do Sprints.**

- Do sprints on the sidewalk in front of your daughter's ballet studio.
- Do sprints right before you eat your packed lunch at work.
- Do sprints in between college classes.
- Do sprints at the park while your kids play.
- Do sprints in front of your house just before bed.
- Do sprints wherever you are.

**Four: Sprints can be Done Almost Anywhere.**

Sprints can give you a boost of energy by releasing endorphins, improving your mood and giving you energy. Instead of looking through social media for 20 minutes, why not listen to music and run some sprints.

To check your pulse, put your index and middle fingers on your neck to the side of your windpipe. When you feel your pulse on your carotid artery, look at your watch and count the number of beats in 10 seconds. Multiply this number by 6 to get your heart rate per minute.

I like to check my pulse right when I finish a sprint and turn around to walk back to the starting point. You will be amazed at how a few sets of sprints a week added to your exercise regimen can help you drop weight quickly. Sprints can also be the catalyst of a new workout lifestyle for your journey to a healthier you. You may not feel very fast at first, but don't sweat it. As long as you're hitting your target heart rate, you are accomplishing your fitness goals of exercising your heart and increasing your metabolism!

**Five: Modify with Low Impact Sprints.**

For a low-impact version of the sprint, try speed walking. You can still get the same great cardio workout with less stress on your joints!

Don't forget that you can do all things—even sprints— through Jesus who gives you strength (Philippians 4.13).

## Target Heart Rate in Beats Per Minute

| Age | Target HR 50-85% | Maximum HR 100% |
|-----|------------------|-----------------|
| 20 | 100-170 | 200 |
| 30 | 95-162 | 190 |
| 35 | 93-157 | 185 |
| 40 | 90-153 | 180 |
| 45 | 88-149 | 175 |
| 50 | 85-145 | 170 |
| 55 | 83-140 | 165 |
| 60 | 80-136 | 160 |
| 65 | 78-132 | 155 |
| 70 | 75-128 | 150 |

# DAY 23

# [5 STEPS TO AVOID DISAPPOINTED]

Have you ever discovered that the thought of something can be more rewarding than the reality of it? Date nights, family vacations, new workout machines, different jobs, fresh kitchen remodels, etc. Many times, we allow our anticipation of something to overshadow the reality of it. But is the grass greener in our minds or do our thoughts tend to wear rose-colored glasses?

Everything can be 100 percent perfect in our imagination. Real life is messy, takes work and comes with difficulty. Our musings can paint moments that are picture-perfect every time. However, if we are not careful, we will let our own expectations cause us to always be disappointed.

The truth is that no person, no moment and no object is perfect. We can learn how to avoid being disappointed and truly enjoy each day with 5 simple steps.

**5 Steps to Avoid Disappointments.**

Disappointments are going to happen in this life. But we can avoid many of them by shifting our own attitudes. We don't want to live our lives wearing the heavy cloak of disappointment because it will cause us to be too weak to stand firm during spiritual attacks and sudden earthly trials. We can shed this heavy cloak with 5 steps.

**Step 1: Avoid Perfectionism.**

People who expect perfection will ALWAYS be disappointed. Instead of expecting 100% all the time, it's best to offer a buffer of grace. Perfection is truly a subjective term. What we think is perfect may be someone else's not-good-enough and vice versa. When our lives are full of grace, we won't be disappointed so much. Grace simply means focusing on the good of a person or situation instead of the bad.

> "May the grace of the Lord Jesus be with God's holy people" (Revelation 22.21 NLT).

**Step 2: Avoid Over-Thinking.**

There is nothing wrong with anticipating and musing about future events. However, we must remember that today is just as special as any day. Each day is a gift from God. When we over-think a future event, our heads are not in the here and now, and we'll miss special moments happening all around us. Yes, we can plan and get excited, but our anticipation of a moment should never become more relevant than the actual moment.

> "This is the day the Lord has made. We will rejoice and be glad in it" (Psalm 118.24 NKJV).

**Step 3: Avoid Self-Focused Thoughts.**

Life does not revolve around us. There are other people and circumstances that surround us each day. Also, God has His ultimate Kingdom Plan that we want to be a part of. When we constantly think about our own desires and plans, we cut out the desires and plans of others, including God. We can avoid being disappointed when we allow our thoughts to be shaped by our love for God and our love for others.

> "Don't be selfish; don't try to impress others. Be humble, thinking of others as better than yourselves" (Philippians 2.3 NLT).

**Step 4: Avoid Over-Planning.**

It's good to have a blueprint of what we expect and want. But we should leave plenty of room for surprises and change. Our anticipation for enjoying the moment and the people around us should override any stringent plan we could devise. If we are too rigid with our planning, we will lack compassion and miss many beautiful moments. Jesus demonstrated this compassion when He altered the "blueprint" of His agenda because of His love for others.

> "When he saw the crowds, he had compassion on them because they were confused and helpless, like sheep without a shepherd" (Matthew 9.36 NLT).

**Step 5: Avoid Over-Controlling.**

Controlling people can be easily disappointed when people aren't doing exactly what they say and when situations aren't exactly how they want them. But what controlling people don't realize is that it's exhausting having to be in charge all the time. We limit our capacity when we micromanage because there is only so much we can control without falling apart. Sometimes God calls us to the front seat, but other times He calls us to sit in the back and let others lead. Both situations can be rewarding.

"You can make many plans, but the Lord's purpose will prevail" (Proverbs 19.21 NLT).

# DAY 24

## [5 HABITS TO HEAR FROM GOD]

Hearing from God consistently doesn't happen overnight. Yes, God is always speaking to us through the Bible, other people, nature and circumstances. He is all around us in heaven and earth (Jeremiah 23.23-24). He also speaks to us directly since His Spirit resides within us (Romans 8.9).

However, our spiritual ears and eyes need time to develop. When we accept Jesus as our Lord and Savior, we in essence become like newborn babies. We must grow in our faith as we learn to listen to the still, soft voice of God (1 Kings 19.12). Many people become frustrated because they either don't think God is speaking or they can't discern His voice. Like learning any new skill, though, it will take time and we will make mistakes.

We can extend grace to ourselves knowing that every day is a new chance to grow. Plus, we can give ourselves room to make mistakes without feeling defeated. Learning to hear God is a process. Nothing valuable happens overnight, and hearing from God is simply part of growing up in the faith (Ephesians 4.15 NIV).

The following are 5 habits to help you hear from God as you grow spiritually in Christ.

"Trust God from the bottom of your heart; don't try to figure out everything on your own. Listen for God's voice in everything you do, everywhere you go; he's the one who will keep you on track. Don't assume that you know it all..." (Proverbs 3.6 MSG).

## How to Hear from God: Habit 1 – ASK.

First things first. Ask God in Jesus' name to help you hear His voice. God allowed His Son, Jesus, to die for us, so He could have a relationship with us. He wants us to hear Him. When we pray anything according to God's will, we know that He will answer our prayer request (John 14.13 NIV). All we need to do is ask, and God will open our ears to Him.

> "I love the Lord, for he heard my voice; he heard my cry for mercy. Because he turned his ear to me, I will call on him as long as I live" (Psalm 116.1-2 NIV).

## How to Hear from God: Habit 2 – SLOW.

Rushing is a sure-fire way to miss God's voice. How many times have we regretted actions because we jumped ahead without thinking? God is continually speaking to us, and He has words of wisdom to share with us. As we learn to slow down, we will become better and better at hearing God.

> "He says, 'Be still, and know that I am God; I will be exalted among the nations, I will be exalted in the earth'" (Psalm 46.10 NIV).

## How to Hear from God: Habit 3 – READ.

Reading helps us learn God's language. It is hard to hear God if we aren't accustomed to His Words. As we read (or listen) to the Bible and other biblical resources, our spiritual language will become richer and more versed. We will better hear from God when His words are in our heart.

> "I have hidden your word in my heart, that I might not sin against you" (Psalm 119.11 NLT).

**How to Hear from God: Habit 4 – PRAY.**

Opening dialogue with God will help us hear from Him more. When we go to pray, it is an invitation to God to join us for a time of communication and intimacy. We can pray to God and then listen for His reply. As we pray every day, we will get better and better at hearing God's voice.

> "In the morning, Lord, you hear my voice; in the morning I lay my requests before you and wait expectantly" (Psalm 5.3 NIV).

**How to Hear from God: Habit 5 – WAIT.**

Waiting is a very undervalued skill. We think idle time is a waste of time. However, waiting patiently for God to speak opens a supernatural world of possibilities. Waiting shows God that we earnestly desire to hear from Him. Time spent away from distractions to wait on God will develop our spiritual ears to hear from God.

> "Wait patiently for the Lord. Be brave and courageous. Yes, wait patiently for the Lord" (Psalm 27.14 NLT).

# DAY 25

## [5 REASONS TO STOP OVERANALYZING YOURSELF]

"Examine yourselves to see if your faith is genuine. Test yourselves. Surely you know that Jesus Christ is among you; if not, you have failed the test of genuine faith" (2 Corinthians 13.5 NLT).

**Who are the People Who Overanalyze?**

There are some people who don't struggle with over-analyzing themselves. They make decisions and press forward without a moment's hesitation or doubt. Their focus is on the world outside of them and inward reflection is not something they spend time doing. The only time they do stop and consider their actions is when someone they value says something. This article is not for those people. This article is for those of us on the opposite side of the spectrum where self-analysis creates fear and doubt, crippling us from moving forward in our destiny.

**Having an Over-Analyzing Overdose.**

The Bible is very clear that we should examine our actions. It is healthy to take time throughout the day to examine our heart and intentions and see whether love is the springboard of everything we do. However, there are a few of us who overdose on self-analysis to the point that we will ALWAYS fall short, we will NEVER be good enough and we

CONTINUALLY make mistakes. Thus, the predicament of human nature.

When we find ourselves focusing more on our flaws than the forgiveness and grace of Jesus Christ, we have fallen into sin. The sin of over-analyzing is so prevalent because we have a mistaken belief that it is good. But it is not. In fact, over-analysis is a slow drip of poison coming from the lying syringe of Satan himself. Therefore, I want to expose that evil poison for what it is: Satan's attempt to make us so consumed by our imperfections and failings that we will never live out the best life that God has for us.

The problem is that many of us have created so many pathways in our mind that lead to over-analysis that we have difficulty creating pathways of grace, mercy and freedom. But let me help you as I helped myself. Here are my 5 Reasons found in God's Word to stop over-analyzing yourself.

**Reason 1: Jesus Loves You.**

I know this reason sounds basic, yet it is so powerful that it can transform your life. When you are surrounded by the love of God, there is no room for negative thoughts. Anytime you begin to fall into a deep pit of over-analyzing yourself, lean into God's presence and His Word. He has so much love, care and tenderness that He wants to pour over your life. He accepts you completely as you are with imperfections and flaws, and He always see the best in you.

> "I have loved you even as the Father has loved me. Remain in my love" (John 15.9 NLT).

**Reason 2: Jesus Forgives You.**

Forgiven means completely made right. Your past, present and future mistakes have all been erased by the blood of Jesus if you accept Him as your Lord and Savior. His mercies are continually washing over your life (Lamentations 3.22-23). This truth should overshadow our mistakes. Jesus' Blood is way more powerful than our regrets.

> "Bear with each other and forgive one another if any of you has a grievance against someone. Forgive as the Lord forgave you" (Colossians 3.13 NIV).

**Reason 3: Jesus Redeems You.**

Jesus not only redeems our spirit, but He redeems our every second of every day. On Sabbath (the 7th Day of Creation) God rested knowing that Jesus' Finished Work on the Cross would redeem the entire earth back to God (Genesis 2.2-3). We can run our race to win (1 Corinthians 9.24), knowing that Jesus redeems and perfects all our steps done in obedience to Him (Colossians 1.20). You don't have to be perfect – just believe that Jesus redeems everything.

> "In him we have redemption through his blood, the forgiveness of sins, in accordance with the riches of God's grace" (Ephesians 1.7 NIV).

**Reason 4: Jesus Gives You His Perfection.**

We have been made right in God's eyes (Romans 5.1). Proof of that truth is the Indwelling of the Holy Spirit. God uses this life to work that supernatural perfection into our natural lives. We can't let our little slip-ups throw us off the path that God has laid out for us. If God sees you as perfected, you must walk confidently in that truth. No more dwelling on mistakes that have already been forgiven and are here no more.

> "For by one sacrifice he has made perfect forever those who are being made holy" (Hebrews 10.14 NIV).

**Reason 5: Jesus Pleads for You.**

Pleading on our behalf shows that Jesus not only loves us, but He is also rooting for us. Jesus lived in this world and wore flesh just like we do. He understands our temptations and knows first-hand what we are going through (Hebrews 4.15) We don't have to over-analyze; rather, we can recognize where we went wrong and give the situation back to God's care. Plus, we can trust that Jesus is ALWAYS on our side, encouraging us, praying for us and cheering us on.

> "Who then will condemn us? No one—for Christ Jesus died for us and was raised to life for us, and he is sitting in the place of honor at God's right hand, pleading for us" (Romans 8.34 NLT).

# DAY 26

# [3 REASONS WHY WE NEED JESUS]

"Instead, you must worship Christ as Lord of your life. And if someone asks about your hope as a believer, always be ready to explain it" (1 Peter 3.15 NLT).

**Why Do We Need Jesus?**

Knowledge fosters faith. The more we know about who Jesus is and His purposes on earth and in our lives, the fuller our faith will become. The fuller our faith becomes, the easier it becomes to walk in our destiny.

Jesus is the merging point of our natural and supernatural lives. He is the starting point of all things eternal in the presence of God. Hell is the absence of God. Heaven is the presence of God. We are separated from God because we can't be perfect and holy. We demanded the Commandments (Exodus 19.8), yet still we failed to be perfect. Therefore, God's justice and love collide in the sacrifice of Jesus on the Cross.

"This is real love—not that we loved God, but that he loved us and sent his Son as a sacrifice to take away our sins" (1 John 4.10 NLT).

We can be in God's presence even in our imperfect state because of the Finished Work of Jesus on the Cross. Jesus allowed Himself to be born into flesh. Then He lived a perfect human life and died for the sins of humanity. Jesus gives us His perfection and takes our sin (1 Peter 2.24), so we have been made right with God through Christ (Romans 5.1). Now we can be in the presence of God.

First, God gives us the Holy Spirit while we are on this earth, so we can have a Helper (Acts 2.38). Second, we enter heaven (the presence of God) once our bodies die (Romans 6.23). All sin has been placed on Jesus; therefore, all life is given through Him. He is the ONLY way to have eternal life with God (John 14.6). Human-centric, try-to-be-good-enough efforts will get us nowhere. The following are 3 reasons why we need Jesus.

> "Salvation is found in no one else, for there is no other name under heaven given to mankind by which we must be saved" (Acts 4.12 NIV).

**Reason 1: Jesus is not a Religion.**

Throughout time, people have tried to organize systems to gain God's love and entrance to His presence. God loves us unconditionally even when we were still sinners (Romans 5.8). He is the embodiment of love and extends love to us freely because we are His creation and made in His image (Genesis 1.27).

We could never gain access to God in our own strength. We all fall short of God's holiness (Romans 3.23). Therefore, Christianity is not a religion; it is a faith. Jesus is the Person of God sent to the earth to save us and bring us back to God. All we must do is believe and receive salvation by faith because of God's grace (Ephesians 2.8-9). This is the first reason why we need Jesus.

> "If you openly declare that Jesus is Lord and believe in your heart that God raised him from the dead, you will be saved. For it is by believing in your heart that you are made right with God, and it is by openly declaring your faith that you are saved" (Romans 10.9-10 NLT).

**Reason 2: Jesus is the Only Way.**

If there were another way to achieve perfection and attain access to God's presence, Jesus would not have had to die (Matthew 26.39). Jesus allowed Himself to be forsaken by God, taking on the sins of the world thereby removing Himself from the very presence of a holy God. Jesus obeyed this path of separation, so we would never have to be forsaken or separated from God (Deuteronomy 31:6). Jesus cried out only one sentence while dying for us on the Cross: "My God, My God, why have You forsaken Me?" (Matthew 27.46 NKJV).

For the first time in His eternal existence, Jesus was separated from God. And, finally, we could be joined to Him even in our imperfect state. However, Jesus had the power to lay down His life, and He had the power to take it back up again. He carried our sin to death and resurrected Himself, leaving our sin behind. All our sins have been left in the tomb, and we can now have life in Christ with God because of Jesus' sacrifice (John 14.20). This is the second reason why we need Jesus.

"No one takes it from Me, but I lay it down of Myself. I have power to lay it down, and I have power to take it again. This command I have received from My Father" (John 10.18 NKJV).

**Reason 3: Jesus is God with Us.**

Jesus is God in the flesh (1 Timothy 3.16). Many movies show the hero entering the world of those whom he or she will save: *Avatar, Superman, Dances with Wolves, Gorillas in the Mist*, etc. The hero must enter the world and become like the ones needing help to save them. Jesus is Living Water rained down on the earth mixed with flesh and squeezed out on time and history in order to perfect and reconcile the world and its people back to God. Jesus' Blood is literally God in the flesh – the life essence of our Creator – covering the earth to redeem it. Jesus had to become like us to save us.

After Jesus gave up His Spirit on the Cross, His side was pierced and both water and blood came out (John 19.34). Water represents the Spirit. Blood represents flesh. Jesus is God in the flesh, pouring out His blood to save the earth. Jesus is literally the Person of God who entered our earth, becoming like us in order to save us (Matthew 1.23). We can now have God's Spirit with us – no matter how we fall short – because of Jesus' sacrifice on the Cross. This is the third reason why we need Jesus.

"He put aside everything that belonged to Him and made Himself the same as a servant who is owned by someone. He became human by being born as a man. After He became a man, He gave up His

134

important place and obeyed by dying on a cross"
(Philippians 2.7-8 NLV).

# DAY 27

# [8 WAYS TO RENEW YOUR HEART]

**You Can Have a Renaissance Washing for Your Heart.**

> "But when the kindness and love of God our Savior appeared, he saved us, not because of righteous things we had done, but because of his mercy. He saved us through the washing of rebirth and renewal by the Holy Spirit, whom he poured out on us generously through Jesus Christ our Savior, so that, having been justified by his grace, we might become heirs having the hope of eternal life" (Titus 3.4-7 NIV).

The Renaissance Period was a time between the 14th to 17th century when a rebirth of art, literature and music took place. The word, *renaissance*, means a revival or a renewed interest in something, and its synonyms include Rebirth, Revival, Renewal, Reawakening, Regeneration.

When we feel our faith has grown stagnant and our hearts are not bathed in God's love, we may need a Renaissance Washing. The joy of God is so bright and amazing. The fact that the Holy Spirit walks this life with us produces awe in the deepest parts of our souls. To forget the miracle of mercy is to vanquish all joy and peace of life. God always wants to revive our heart and renew our first love in Him.

"Yet I hold this against you: You have forsaken the love you had at first" (Revelation 2.4 NIV).

## Do We Have a Distracted Heart?

Rebirth begins on our Salvation Day, the day we ask Jesus Christ to be our Lord and Savior. But just like the ocean, the waves of renewal should wash over us continuously. Each wave bathes our heart and brings us into greater intimacy with God. The enemy to this washing is distraction brought on by worries and greed. When we worry, we reveal our mistrust of God. When we covet, we reveal a discontented heart. These distractions prevent us from dipping into the basin of His Living Water where we find refreshment and renewal for our inner person.

> "The seed falling among the thorns refers to someone who hears the word, but the worries of this life and the deceitfulness of wealth choke the word, making it unfruitful" (Matthew 13.22 NIV).

## 8 Ways to Renew your Heart.

When I feel like I've forgotten the mystery, the beauty and the awe-inspiring goodness of God, I know that I need to do something to immerse myself in His presence, so the waves of His mercy and grace can wash over my hardening heart. The Holy Spirit is God's gift to us in an imperfect world Who came at the price of God's Son, Jesus. I want to open that gift and allow it to permeate my thoughts, attitude, emotions, actions and day. It's interesting how we will give ourselves wholly to worry, entertainment, relationships and pleasures, but we have difficulty giving ourselves completely to the majesty and tenderness of God. When I feel my heart has become distracted and cold, I aggressively want to wake it up.

> "This is why it is said: 'Wake up, sleeper, rise from the dead, and Christ will shine on you'" (Ephesians 5.14 NIV).

**Heart Renewal 1: Seek a New Perspective.**

Our faith grows stagnant when we arrive at the end of ourselves. We must seek other spiritual voices via podcasts, books, sermons and relationships. These unique points of view offer us a more dynamic and fuller view of God and His love for us.

Right now I am studying the early Celtic Christians just after St. Patrick revived their world with the presence of God the Father, Son and Holy Spirit. The Celtic Christians died young, and infant mortality was very high. They didn't know if they would make it through the night, let alone until they were 80 years old. The briefness of their lives caused them to have a profound joy in the present moment and a deep appreciation of Jesus' love and sacrifice for them. My soul is refreshed when my perspective aligns with a new revelation of God's goodness.

**Heart Renewal 2: Start Something New.**

Doing a new activity creates a childlike atmosphere of learning and growth in our lives. We can get comfortable where we are and avoid taking risks. I always tell my kids that "You have to be bad at something before you can be good at it." The problem is that we have become so entitled that we view starting something new as a pain in the neck rather than a new adventure.

I have made it a lifestyle choice to always learn and try new things. Currently, I am learning how to cook gourmet meals. During over 22 years of marriage, I have always been the main cook of the family. However, in the last few years, I've desired my meals to be restaurant worthy. I host people at my home several times a month, so I want my entrees to be delicious and beautiful. This creative process gives me a deeper appreciation of God's gift of food, creativity and hospitality.

**Heart Renewal 3: Serve Others.**

Serving others is the quickest and surest way to have a spiritual revival. We are endowed with purpose, and too many self-serving activities can leave us feeling useless and meaningless. Although there is nothing wrong with self-care, there should always be areas in our lives that we give of ourselves freely without expectation of award or acclaim.

One example of serving in my private life is that I enjoy packing up leftovers for family and friends. I try to make extra every time I bake or cook, so at least one other person can enjoy a home-cooked meal or dessert. An example in my public life is that I make it a priority to read other writers' books and give them a review on my blog and Amazon. Reviews are very important to writers. These words of encouragement and affirmation highlight their long hours of working in the shadows.

**Heart Renewal 4: Tune Out the World.**

The world produces so many little roots that entangle us each day. From social media to emails to home and work responsibilities – our focus is constantly being pulled into the natural world with little time to spare for spiritual matters. We have to make a choice to set our computers, TVs and phones aside to bathe in the reviving presence of God. And we can't simply do five minutes and expect to have a hearty, full experience with the Father. He wants to engage with us, and it takes time for our distracted thoughts to slowly turn toward Him.

If I don't spend time with God each day, I know that I'll hit the floor running with my keyboard on my lap and my phone in my hand. However, some days I need more than just a quiet time in the morning. When I sense that I need to spend a big chunk of time with God, I will either take a bath or take a walk. The bath helps me to really focus my attention on God because the distractions of the world are momentarily shut away. A walk outside also allows me to listen to His voice while enjoying His creations – nature, birds, wind, etc.

**Heart Renewal 5: Record God's Promises.**

The Bible is filled with God's Promises. God will highlight verses and apply them to our lives. We can write these promises down and read them whenever we feel like our faith is running low. Also, God will give us special words from people we trust. We can write these words of encouragement down and read over them if we are struggling with doubts and fears.

I have many verses highlighted in my Bible that God has given me at just the right time. Currently, I'm in a season where He's been giving me the same dozen or so verses over and over again. I have used colored tabs to mark them in my Bible. Whenever I feel doubt creeping in, I grab my Bible and reread these verses. The words remind me of the promises of hope God has given me.

**Heart Renewal 6: Create Something New.**

God is a Creator God and He made us in His image. We were designed to be creators. This doesn't mean we have to create art, literature or music. We can simply create a meal, a prayer, a conversation, an act of service.... When we ignite our God-given imagination, there is no limit to what we can do in Christ. Much of our stagnation is due to our limited expression of God's love and goodness in our lives. God is unlimited, and we can tap into His imagination to create something beautiful.

Something I like to create is an imaginative time of prayer with God. Reading the Bible has fueled my imagination with many images that paint the supernatural world in my mind. I imagine myself in the throne room of God. I see myself wearing the Armor of God: the Helmet of Salvation, the Breastplate of Righteousness, the Belt of Truth, the Shield of Faith, the Shoes of Peace and the Sword of the Spirit (Ephesians 6.10-17 NIV). And I stand as a warrior princess, pledging my full allegiance to the Lord of lords and King of kings.

**Heart Renewal 7: Read Scripture Aloud.**

The Bible is very specific on the power of spoken words. Reading the Word (which is Jesus in the flesh) out loud will have powerful effects on our lives (John 1.1). The enemy hates the Bible because he knows the Bible contains the energy of our Living God. When we feel like we are slipping into defeat, we can take up our Bibles (Swords of the Spirit) and wield out slicing words that gain ground for God and take territory from the devil.

I have a Bible app that reads the Bible to me. When I'm struggling with melancholy emotions, I take my phone and play my Bible. If I wake up with dark feelings, I'll listen. If I'm wrestling with doubt, I'll listen. If my heart feels despondent, I'll listen. The Bible is living and active, and it is sharp enough to cut away all thoughts and feelings that are not of God (Hebrews 4.12).

**Heart Renewal 8: Do a Daily Devotional.**

Daily devotionals sometimes get very little credit for how much purpose they can serve. The writer of each devotional is like a chef who prepares a delicious meal or a scrumptious dessert from the ingredients within the Bible. Although reading the Bible for ourselves is very important, sometimes we need to sit at someone else's table and feast on what they've prepared. Daily Devotionals usually don't greatly impact us in a single moment (although they can); rather, it is the day-by-day nourishment that feeds us over time.

I've read so many daily devotionals that it is impossible to list them all, but a few of them are *My Utmost for His Highest*, *Streams in the Desert*, *Sparkling Gems from the Greek*, *Jesus Calling* and my one-year devotional, Slay the *Day*. Whenever I open one of these daily devotionals, God always speaks to me. My life and current situations may be different from what I'm reading, but there is an eternal principle that can be applied to my life at the moment.

# DAY 28

# [4 REMINDERS OF WHO YOU ARE IN CHRIST]

**Who You are in Christ.**

Many people are saved by the Blood of Jesus Christ through His Finished Work on the Cross. However, they may not know their true identity in Christ once they become saved. Also, some people gain a growing understanding of who they are in Christ, yet the world tries to make them forget. We get bogged down by responsibility and worry. Or we get distracted by covetousness and insecurity. And we lose sight of who God created us to be. But when we fully embrace who we are in Christ each day, we will find the purpose and peace our soul craves.

No matter how we feel or what the world says, we must remember two things: God created you, and He created you with purpose.

**5 Reminders of Who You are in Christ.**

Whenever we feel negative emotions bombarding our thoughts and beliefs, we need to align our eyes with heaven.

> "Think about the things of heaven, not the things of earth" (Colossians 3.2 NLT).

144

As we continually bring the truth of our identity into our thoughts, we will begin to believe what the Bible says about us. We must learn to see through God's eyes and not from our own distorted viewpoint. Only when we can see our true identity in Christ, will we be able to live in God's powerful purpose.

**Reminder 1: You Reflect the Image of God.**

> "So God created human beings in his own image. In the image of God he created them; male and female he created them" (Genesis 1.27 NLT).

This is enough truth to fill our hearts with so much gratitude and awe. God, the Creator of the Universe, created us – both men and women – in His image. We have all of God's glory, beauty, creativity and authority woven into the very fibers of our being. We have a fountain of God's goodness within us that only Jesus can reveal. Whenever we feel unworthy or less than, we can remind ourselves that we are made in the image of a Holy God.

**Reminder 2: You are a Masterpiece.**

> "For we are God's masterpiece. He has created us anew in Christ Jesus, so we can do the good things he planned for us long ago" (Ephesians 2.10 NLT).

A masterpiece is a one-of-a-kind creation that is priceless. How many times do we feel like we are just average and nothing special? But that is not what the Bible says. God has placed great value into us. In fact, we have so much value that God died for each of us (Romans 5.8). Someone worth dying for must be valued and loved!

### Reminder 3: You are a Child of God.

> "For you are all children of God through faith in Christ Jesus. And all who have been united with Christ in baptism have put on Christ, like putting on new clothes" (Galatians 3.26-27 NLT).

Sometimes we don't fully grasp what it means to be God's child. As God's children, we inherit His Kingdom. We are royalty. We may watch earthly royalty on TV or see them on the cover of magazines, but we are eternal royalty – princes and princesses forever. We should walk with the confidence of our royal birthright by faith, not because the world says so but because the King of the Universe does.

### Reminder 4: You are a Holy Priest.

> "But you are not like that, for you are a chosen people. You are royal priests, a holy nation, God's very own possession. As a result, you can show others the goodness of God, for he called you out of the darkness into his wonderful light" (1 Peter 2.9 NLT).

Who are the priests? They are those called to do the work of God. God has a great destiny for each of us. Our very lives have great meaning in the world around us. Every moment is saturated with value and purpose. We find our purpose as we seek God daily. He will lead us into our full potential on earth as it is already recorded in heaven.

### Reminder 5: You are Co-heirs with Christ.

"And since we are his children, we are his heirs. In fact, together with Christ we are heirs of God's glory. But if we are to share his glory, we must also share his suffering" (Romans 8.17 NLT).

Jesus is the Son of God, and because of His great love and grace, He has seated us with Him at the right-hand side of God (Ephesians 2.6). Therefore, everything that Jesus has, we have. Everything that Jesus does, we can do. We have so much authority in Christ, and the devil does not want us to discover it. But we can take the Bible at its Word, we are co-heirs—equal partners—with Christ.

# DAY 29

## [11 REASONS TO READ YOUR BIBLE]

> "I will study your commandments and reflect on your ways. I will delight in your decrees and not forget your word" (Psalm 119.15-16 NLT).

I tell people often that I read the Bible because I know how valuable it is to my entire life. It is literally like water to my spirit. And since my spirit is eternal, it supersedes and shapes my natural being as well – body and soul (mind, emotions and will). I read God's Word because it gives me energy, clears my mind, directs my path, draws me to God, abates my worries and satisfies my soul.

**Read the Bible for Guidance.**

If God can direct the universe, then He can direct our lives through our Bible reading time. Reading the Owner's Manual to Life (the Bible) is the only way to live life at its best design.

> "Your word is a lamp to guide my feet and a light for my path" (Psalm 119.105 NLT).

**Read the Bible for Sustenance.**

We are both physical and spiritual beings, so we need natural food and supernatural food to stay strong and healthy. Also, during difficult seasons in life, we may need a lot of spiritual nourishment. Reading your Bible provides that necessary nourishment.

> "People do not live by bread alone, but by every word that comes from the mouth of God" (Matthew 4.4 NLT).

**Read the Bible because it's Alive.**

The Bible is not only a physical book but also a supernatural Source of Good. It is God's Living Water (His Presence) moving through our lives (John 7.38) as we read it. Read the Bible and pour God's energy into your life.

> "For the word of God is alive and powerful. It is sharper than the sharpest two-edged sword, cutting between soul and spirit, between joint and marrow. It exposes our innermost thoughts and desires" (Hebrews 4.12 NLT).

**Read the Bible for Blessing**.

Reading the Bible promotes wellness in our lives as we allow it to shape our beliefs, thoughts and actions. We may not feel the results of its nourishment at first, but our daily reading will eventually become evident.

> "God blesses the one who reads the words of this prophecy to the church, and he blesses all who listen to its message and obey what it says..." (Revelation 1.3 NLT).

**Read the Bible to Purify.**

Reading the Bible is to the spirit like water is to the body, it purifies! Reading your Bible gets rid of all the spiritual toxins (doubt, worry, fear, etc.) and replaces it with pure liquid Jesus and all that good found in Him. Read your Bible and feel refreshed and revived.

> "How can a young man cleanse his way? By taking heed according to Your word" (Psalm 119.9 NKJV).

**Read the Bible for Correction and Equipping.**

We can live in victory because the Bible is pruning all that is not of God and replacing it with things that help us overcome. Letting God correct us by reading the Bible leaves room for Him to equip and provide for us.

> "All Scripture is inspired by God and is useful to teach us what is true and to make us realize what is wrong in our lives. It corrects us when we are wrong and teaches us to do what is right. God uses it to prepare and equip his people to do every good work" (2 Timothy 3.16-17 NLT).

**Read the Bible for More Jesus**.

The Bible says that Jesus is the Word spoken to create and redeem all of us. Jesus is the Person of God in the flesh, and His presence flows in the Bible. When we read the Bible, we drink the very presence of Jesus and all that good contained in Him.

> "In the beginning the Word already existed. The Word was with God, and the Word was God. He existed in the beginning with God. God created

everything through him, and nothing was created except through him" (John 1.1-3 NLT)

**Read the Bible for Healing**.

The well-spring of Jesus' healing power is found in the Bible. Once we fully believe God and His promises found in His Word, our faith WILL activate Jesus' power in our spiritual, physical, relational, emotional and mental lives. We just need to read our Bible to get that power.

> "He personally carried our sins in his body on the cross so that we can be dead to sin and live for what is right. By his wounds you are healed" (1 Peter 2.24 NLT).

**Read the Bible because it's your Offensive Weapon**.

God protects us, but He does give us one tool to fight back and to overcome, the Bible! Reading the Bible every day will make us more skilled at wielding our Swords and fighting the good fight of faith (2 Timothy 4.7-8). We can only have victory each day by reading the Bible.

> "Put on salvation as your helmet, and take the sword of the Spirit, which is the word of God" (Ephesians 6.17 NLT).

**Read the Bible because it's Freedom**.

If we feel oppressed by thoughts or limited by our own attitudes, the Bible is Truth. And once we know the truth about who we are in Christ by reading the Bible, we will live in the freedom that God has given us as His children and co-heirs with Christ (Romans 8.17). Read the Bible and walk in complete freedom.

> "And you will know the truth, and the truth will set you free" (John 8.32 NLT).

**Read the Bible because it's Eternal.**

Every promise the Bible gives us as we read it each day stays with us forever. Everything in this world will fade except those things rooted in Christ. Read the Bible and discover what's eternal, so you can apply eternity to your daily life on earth.

> "Heaven and earth will disappear, but my words will never disappear" (Matthew 24.35 NLT).

# DAY 30

# [10 BENEFITS OF JUMP ROPING]

**A History of Jumping Rope.**

Jumping rope has been around since ancient times. Historians believe that jumping rope may have started with Egyptians using vines. However, the jump rope did not become widely popular until the early 1900s. Jumping rope became distinctly popular in the inner cities during the 1940s and 1950s because it was an inexpensive pass time for kids.

**Benefits of Jumping Rope are Numerous.**

**One, jumping rope can be done anywhere.** You don't have to leave the house or purchase an expensive machine to exercise. Moreover, when you go on vacation, the jump rope is easy to take with you.

**Two, jumping rope has less impact**. Jumping rope is easier on the knees and ankles than other cardio exercises because the jumper lands on the balls of the feet. This absorbs and disperses the impact.

**Three, jumping rope is a full body workout**. The arms, legs, core, back and heart – almost every muscle in the body activates when jumping rope.

**Four, jumping rope helps with coordination.** Your brain needs to keep track of the rotation of the arms

153

simultaneously with the jumping of the feet. This elevated focus greatly benefits all the jumper's other physical activities.

**Five, jumping rope is a major calorie burn.** Jumping rope is a cardio compound exercise engaging all muscles. The heart and metabolism will have to pick up the pace to keep up. With the extra calorie burn, fat will begin to disappear.

**Six, jumping rope increases bone density.** The subtle impact that the bones do receive will safely increase bone density. This will help the jumper maintain bone strength as he or she ages.

**Seven, jumping rope is extremely inexpensive.** With a cost of only $15-$30, the jump rope will more than pay for its initial investment.

**Eight, jumping rope is good for both beginning and advanced fitness levels.** The speed of jumping rope is completely up to the jumper. Beginning levels can jump slowly. While advanced levels can jump quickly.

**Nine, jumping rope is a time saver.** From 15 minutes to 25 minutes, you can get a full body and cardiovascular workout in less time.

**Ten, jumping rope is a great warmup.** Before throwing around the weights, jumping rope can warmup all the muscles including the heart. It can also be used in between weightlifting sets to keep the heart strong and the metabolism burning.

**Jumping Rope to Burn Fat.**

Jumping rope will help you lose weight fast. Because it is a high-intensity compound exercise, your body will drop weight in only 20 minutes a day. Jumping rope has been a staple for professional fighters since before the *Rocky* movies. Fighters must last several 5-minute rounds in the ring or cage. They use the compound high-intensity exercise of jumping rope to get their stamina up to par. It will effectively help you to drop the weight and get you ready to fight the good fight of faith.

> "Fight the good fight of faith. Take hold of the life that lasts forever. You were chosen to receive it. You have spoken well about this life in front of many people" (1 Timothy 6.12 NLV).

**Jumping Rope Length Measurement.**

- Use a 7-foot jump rope if you are under 4'10"
- Use an 8-foot jump rope if you are between 4'11" and 5'3"
- Use a 9-foot jump rope if you are between 5'4" and 5'10"
- Use a 10-foot jump rope if you are over 5'10"

**Jumping Rope for Beginning Fitness Levels.**

1-minute Jumping Rope:

Beginners or people with moderate arm strength can use a non-weighted jump rope. Start with a 1-minute set of jumping rope. Then march in place for 2 minutes. Do another 1-minute set of jumping rope with another 2-minute march. Repeat this 5 times for a quick, cardio-boosting 15-minute workout.

2-minute Jumping Rope:

Once your body and heart become stronger with more stamina, you can now switch to a 2-minute set of jumping rope. Start with a 2-minute set of jumping rope. Then march in place for 2 minutes. Do another 2-minute set of jumping rope with another 2-minute march. Repeat this 5 times for a quick, cardio-boosting 20-minute workout.

**Jumping Rope for Advanced Fitness Levels.**

3-minute Jumping Rope:

Advanced fitness levels can use weighted jump ropes with 1-pound handles. This will really work the arms, shoulders and upper back. Start with a 3-minute set of jumping rope. Then do 1 minute of squats and 1 minute of lunges. Next, do a 3-minute set of jumping rope. Then do 1 minute of pushups (on toes or knees) and one minute plank. Repeat both sets once for a 20-minute workout or twice for a 30-minute workout.

5-minute Jumping Rope:

Once your body and heart become stronger with increased stamina, you can now switch to a 5-minute set of jumping rope. Start with a 5-minute set of jumping rope. Then do 1 minute of squats and 1 minute of lunges. Next, do another 5-minute set of jumping rope. Then do 1 minute of pushups (on toes or knees) and 1-minute plank. Repeat both sets once for a 28-minute workout or twice for a 42-minute workout.

# DAY 31

# [6 STEPS TO PRAY THE LORD'S WAY]

**Learning to pray doesn't have to be difficult.**

The disciples asked Jesus to teach them to pray. Jesus didn't give them an essay or a thesis on prayer. There wasn't a string of expectations or traditions for prayer. He simply gave them an example of prayer with six steps. Therefore, following these 6 easy steps will help you pray the Lord's Way.

**ONE: Pray in Secret.**

There is a time to pray with others, but there is a time to be alone with God. Try to get away with God each day to pray in secret. In the quiet time with the Lord, He can replenish you and prepare you for the day.

> "But when you pray, go into your room, close the door and pray to your Father, who is unseen. Then your Father, who sees what is done in secret, will reward you" (Matthew 6.6).

**TWO: Recognize God's Authority and His Holiness.**

Come to God with an attitude of awe and reverence but also with the deep awareness that you are loved by Him. Prayer is talking with a Perfect Father. Recognizing His authority is also recognizing that power, strength and provision are on your side.

> "Our Father in heaven, hallowed be your name" (Matthew 6.9).

**THREE: Agree with His Kingdom Plan.**

You don't have to stress, feeling like you must hold the entire world on your shoulders. God has big plans for you. Rest in His mighty hands and ask Him for His plans for you. Then agree with those plans and pray them back to Him.

> "Your kingdom come, your will be done, on earth as it is in heaven" (Matthew 6.10).

**FOUR: Know that God will Provide for your Needs.**

God will take care of your physical, emotional and spiritual needs as you learn to trust Him. Fear is the opposite of faith. Pray for your needs and the needs of others and believe that God cares about the details of your life.

> "Give us today our daily bread" (Matthew 6.11).

**FIVE: Forgive Others and Receive Forgiveness.**

Offering forgiveness is a huge part of the Christian lifestyle. People will never be perfect, but God can turn your hurts into His good. Forgive others and yourself quickly, so bitterness doesn't get a foothold. And ask forgiveness when you have messed up.

And forgive us our debts, as we also have forgiven our debtors" (Matthew 6.12).

**SIX: Aggressively Avoid Evil.**

There is evil all around you—movies, books, music, relationships and the Internet can be filled with beauty or ugliness. Pray and ask God if you should veer away from something that is allowing the devil to gain territory in your life. God wants you to walk in freedom, as you come to Him daily to seek out what is for you and what is not for you.

"And lead us not into temptation, but deliver us from the evil one" (Matthew 6.13).

# DAY 32

## [6 MOTIVATORS FOR INNER CHANGE]

**There are Two Types of Change: Outer and Inner.**

Outer change shifts our inner world. We get married, change jobs, move houses, lose a friend, have a baby, etc. An outer change drastically alters our life, forcing us to adjust to our new circumstances. These transitions happen to us, and we have no choice but to cope and adapt.

Inner change shifts our outer world. We alter our time management, thought processes, attitudes, habits, behaviors, etc. Unlike outer change, this transition occurs inside of us, forcing our circumstances to adjust to our will. These transitions happen by choice, and we move our circumstances by activated faith and action.

**Inner Change Creates Outer Shifts.**

Many times, we beg God to change our circumstances, so we can make a transition to a higher level of growth (Hebrews 6.1). However, God knows that the shift must first happen within us. He wants us to change the world around us. This transition can be difficult because it is easy to give up and go back to our old, antiquated way of living. Our determination and belief that God has something better for us must ignite our resolve. Faith becomes our motivator to change, not our circumstances. Inner transitions are the most difficult to produce, but with God all things are possible.

> "Jesus looked at them and said, 'With man this is impossible, but with God all things are possible'" (Matthew 19.26 NIV).

**Motivator 1: Start Small.**

Imagine a chain-linked necklace. From a distance, the necklace looks like one smooth piece of metal, but in actuality it is made up of small, circular links of metal. Inner change is like that. Each choice and action is a link that attaches itself to a long transitional chain that forces our circumstances to shift. Once we see our inner change is made up of smaller pieces, it will be easier to continue adding links to the bigger picture without feeling defeated.

> "Do not despise these small beginnings, for the Lord rejoices to see the work begin..." (Zechariah 4.10 NLT).

**Motivator 2: Make Goals.**

Learn to make daily, weekly, monthly and yearly goals that become gems along the transition you are creating. These smaller goals are unique portions of the ultimate masterpiece God has in mind. Like the saying goes: "How do you eat an elephant? One bite at a time." The bigger the promise, the more links involved, and the longer it will take. Impatience will always destroy change. Great things take time. Learn to live each day as it comes during the transitional process.

> "For we are God's masterpiece. He has created us anew in Christ Jesus, so we can do the good things he planned for us long ago" (Ephesians 2.10 NLT).

**Motivator 3: Be First.**

Your inner transition will affect those around you, but don't expect others to take up the slack of your personal growth. People can help you, but they are not responsible to keep you motivated. Like the saying goes: "The First Guy Through the Wall Always Gets the Bloodiest." You are in essence the first person trying to break through the wall of change to claim new territory. Once others see your victory, they'll see the possibility of inner change in their own life. You will encourage others by claiming victory through Christ and showing everyone that you can overcome (Revelation 12.11).

> "For our light and momentary troubles are achieving for us an eternal glory that far outweighs them all" (2 Corinthians 4.17 NIV).

**Motivator 4: Speak Life.**

Positive self-talk is extremely important during change. You can encourage yourself with the words you think, believe and speak. The Bible has a lot of amazing things to say about you. You are loved, valued and created for a purpose (1 John 3.1, 1 Peter 2.9 & Romans 8.28). You can encourage yourself in the Lord knowing that Jesus believes in you and is always interceding for you (Romans 8.34 NIV). Your thoughts and words can make a path of lights on your journey of change. Don't think or say anything that will lead your transition in the wrong direction (2 Corinthians 10.5).

162

Inner change is difficult, so speak words that enhance the process, not hinder it.

> "The tongue can bring death or life; those who love to talk will reap the consequences" (Proverbs 18.21 NLT).

## Motivator 5: Renew Strength.

Transitions are difficult and tiring because sometimes the light at the end of the tunnel can't be seen. But don't give up. Instead, learn to rest in God and allow Him to renew your strength like the soaring eagles learn to rest on the wind. The wind pushes them up higher and higher as they yield to its force. An unyielded heart is not easily lifted, but a tender heart becomes like clay in the Potter's Hands (Isaiah 64.8). Learn to rest in God, so He can renew your strength when change becomes wearisome.

> "But those who trust in the Lord will find new strength. They will soar high on wings like eagles. They will run and not grow weary. They will walk and not faint" (Isaiah 40.31 NLT).

## Motivator 6: Find Intimacy.

Life is about getting to know God more deeply and transforming into the image of His Son, Jesus. We are only on this earth for a short time, and God uses each day to shape us into the people we are going to be for eternity. God wants to mold you into your best design. But more importantly, God wants to know you intimately, like a Father wants to know His child (1 John 3.1). He enjoys your company and longs to spend time with you. Inner change is an excellent way to lean into God. As you learn to rely on God, you will fall more deeply in love with Him.

> "So all of us who have had that veil removed can see and reflect the glory of the Lord. And the Lord—who is the Spirit—makes us more and more like him as we are changed into his glorious image" (2 Corinthians 3.18 NLT).

# DAY 33

## [11 BIBLE VERSES OF TRUTH TO CLAIM]

The following are eleven verses that I have clung to during difficult times. It is interesting how these verses move from our minds into our hearts during a struggle. Don't forget: On the other side of our struggle is our triumph (2 Corinthians 2.14). The pains we co-labor with Christ will always give birth to more strength, joy, freedom, wisdom and peace.

**Verse 1 – You Can Claim a PEACE OF MIND.**

> "I am leaving you with a gift—peace of mind and heart. And the peace I give is a gift the world cannot give. So don't be troubled or afraid" (John 14.27 NLT).

Jesus promises us peace, and He cannot lie. Even in the storms of life, we can claim the supernatural peace of God given to us through the Finished Work of Jesus. If you don't have peace in your mind or heart (thoughts and emotions), start declaring this truth until the peace of heaven infiltrates your situations and life.

**Verse 2 – You Can Claim VICTORY.**

> "He gives us victory over sin and death through our Lord Jesus Christ" (1 Corinthians 15.57 NLT).

No matter what life and the enemy throw at you, claim the promise that you have the ultimate victory in Christ. Sometimes, we can't see the victory because the waves of trouble are blocking our view. However, trust that the victory is there, and God is at the moment handing it to you.

**Verse 3 – You Can Claim STRENGTH.**

> "For I can do everything through Christ, who gives me strength" (Philippians 4.13 NLT).

You can do everything through the strength that Jesus gives you. But before you start claiming your victory in an area, make sure that the "everything" you're aiming to accomplish is part of God's plans. If God says you can do it, no matter what obstacles come your way, you will achieve your goal.

**Verse 4 – You Can Claim to be FEARLESS.**

> "For God has not given us a spirit of fear and timidity, but of power, love, and self-discipline" (2 Timothy 1.7 NLT).

Fear is the infection that will make you too weak to stand firm against the enemy's attack and the world's trouble. If you feel fear creeping in, do not give it room. Instantly, tell fear to go, and don't allow your imaginations to spin images rooted in fear. Fear may seem reasonable at first, but once the infection of fear takes hold, it will devastate all areas of your life.

**Verse 5 – You Can Claim GOD'S GOODNESS.**

"If imperfect parents know how to lovingly take care of their children and give them what they need, how much more will the perfect heavenly Father give the Holy Spirit's fullness when his children ask him" (Luke 11.13 TPT).

God is good. Once we understand and receive that truth, it will make life's troubles seem like opportunities to grow and receive from the Lord. Whenever you are faced with a difficult situation, don't reiterate the problem. Instead, begin claiming the answer and thanking God for His provision. This adjustment of our perception will lift the weight of worry and replace it with the joy of expectations.

**Verse 6 – You Can Claim PEACE.**

"I have told you all this so that you may have peace in me. Here on earth you will have many trials and sorrows. But take heart, because I have overcome the world" (John 16.33 NLT).

Peace is priceless, and it is ours by God's promise. If peace is not saturating your mind and heart, it is time to get into God's presence. Instead of trying to fill your days with busyness to distract you from your lack of peace, get before God and stay there until He pours out His peace. It may take a while, but keep going to Him with an expectation of His supplied peace.

**Verse 7 – You Can Claim JOY.**

"I have told you these things so that you will be filled with my joy. Yes, your joy will overflow!" (John 15.11 NLT).

Joy is an inside job, not moved by external circumstances. If God says we can have joy no matter what, then it can't be ushered in by outside sources and happenings. Life has its ups and downs, but joy is a constant. Joy is a deep knowing of being loved, valued and cared for by our Creator. This truth causes supernatural joy to burst forth from our innermost being and spread to all areas of our life, despite our circumstances.

**Verse 8 – You Can Claim HEALING.**

> "He heals the brokenhearted and bandages their wounds" (Psalm 147.3 NLT).

Jesus healed physical, emotional and mental illnesses during His time on earth, and He promised us that we would be able to do the same (John 14.12). Regardless of what the world says, we want to always believe God more. If the Bible says we can be healed, we must have faith that this promise is for us too. Fill your days with words of healing. Don't give up. Continue to speak, believe and wait for God's miracle.

**Verse 9 – You Can Claim to be BRAND NEW.**

> "This means that anyone who belongs to Christ has become a new person. The old life is gone; a new life has begun!" (2 Corinthians 5.17 NLT).

Your past had died in Christ. You are now a new creation. Carrying around your past is like carrying around a dead body – heavy, cumbersome and useless. Whenever thoughts of your past come into your mind, replace them with images of all the amazing things you have accomplished in Christ. Over time, your mind will disperse the bad images with the good ones.

## Verse 10 – You Can Claim WHOLENESS.

> "And our own completeness is now found in him. We are completely filled with God as Christ's fullness overflows within us. He is the Head of every kingdom and authority in the universe!" (Colossians 2.10 TPT).

You are not broken or incomplete. You have been stitched together in Christ, and His grace fills in all the cracks. God sees you in Christ, and You are perfect, holy and sanctified in His eyes. Proof of this truth is the indwelling of the Holy Spirit in you. You are complete and whole and no part of you is lacking or damaged.

## Verse 11 – You Can Claim FREEDOM.

> "So now there is no condemnation for those who belong to Christ Jesus. And because you belong to him, the power of the life-giving Spirit has freed you from the power of sin that leads to death" (Romans 8.1-2 NLT).

You are free from sin and condemnation. Once we fully embrace this truth, our life choices and steps will reflect what we believe. The enemy will always try to accuse you, but just remind yourself and all of heaven and earth that there is no condemnation in Christ (Romans 8.1). You live free from bondage because Jesus died to pay for your freedom.

# DAY 34

# [4 WAYS TO REPLACE FINGER POINTING]

"Then you will call, and the Lord will answer; you will cry for help, and he will say: Here am I. If you do away with the yoke of oppression, with the pointing finger and malicious talk" (Isaiah 58.9 NIV).

**Finger-Pointing Hinders God's Power.**

Finger-pointing is not of God, and anything not of God becomes a feeding ground for the enemy. Yes, the Holy Spirit will lead us sometimes to offer correction to others; however, those moments are always done out of love. Finger-pointing, on the other hand, is rooted in pride, insecurity and/or bitterness and does not reveal God's love or His kingdom.

As we mature in Christ, we begin to notice those things in our lives that are not pleasing to Him. In fact, what is not pleasing to Him increasingly becomes not pleasing to us. And the best way to get rid of old habits that stifle the power of God in our lives is to replace them with new habits that release God's power.

**Changing the Habit of Finger-Pointing.**

We have the ability to change old habits. Like any new change, there is a period of adjustment. But transitions don't have to be unpleasant. In fact, we can see change as an adventure to a better place in Christ. As we walk the path of change, we can remember that we aren't lost or confused. God is with us, and we are right where He wants us to be.

**Facts to Remember about Change.**

- Change does not have to be scary.
- We are never alone.
- We are moving to a better place in Christ.
- The life of change is an adventure.

**Replacing Finger-Pointing with Positive Habits.**

We can't just simply get rid of an old habit. We must replace it. The best way to get rid of finger-pointing is to replace it with PRAYER and PRAISE which will unleash God's POWER. Oftentimes, we finger-point because we don't want to take the blame. But if we remember the following three truths, we won't feel the need to constantly defend ourselves.

**Truth 1: We Don't Need to Finger-Point Because God is for Us.**

We don't need to finger-point and try to defend ourselves because we have a Father in heaven who loves us, and He wants the best for us and is always fighting for us. We can rest in His work of defending us, knowing that He will accomplish both His mercy and justice.

> "The Lord will fight for you; you need only to be still" (Exodus 14.14 NIV).

**Truth 2: We Don't Need to Finger-Point Because the World is Not Perfect.**

We live in a fallen world. Sometimes bad things happen and there is simply no one to blame. But we have the assurance of a world (heaven) that will have no more suffering, and we can trust that God can use ALL THINGS (even the hurts and pains of the world) for His good to those who love and trust Him (Romans 8.28).

> "He will wipe every tear from their eyes. There will be no more death or mourning or crying or pain, for the old order of things has passed away" (Revelation 21.4 NIV).

**Truth 3: We Don't Need to Finger-Point Because We All Carry the Blame.**

No one is perfect, and we all need grace. Each one of us falls short of God's holy standard, and Jesus had to die for all of our sins to give us His righteousness (Romans 3.23). Not one of us is blameless, and finger-pointing sets us up as a judge, but only God is the judge. If we want mercy, we must learn to give mercy and not finger-point.

> "There will be no mercy for those who have not shown mercy to others. But if you have been merciful, God will be merciful when he judges you" (James 2.13 NLT).

**One: Replace Finger-Pointing with Prayer.**

When we feel the need to finger-point, we can replace laying blame with prayer. Every time we want to criticize others, we can pray for them. Our prayers show God that we trust Him to be the ultimate judge. Plus, praying will also make us feel better. Carrying around blame is draining and allows the enemy a foothold into our lives, but praying creates unending strength and energy, revitalizing our youth and joy.

> "But those who trust in the Lord will find new strength. They will soar high on wings like eagles. They will run and not grow weary. They will walk and not faint" (Isaiah 40.31 NLT).

**Two: Replace Finger-Pointing with Praise.**

God loves when we praise Him because our joy can be found in the act of praising Him. We can let our urge to finger-point actually become a catalyst for praise. We can flip the script of what the enemy wants us to do by allowing praise to take over. The Bible says that God dwells in the praises of His people. When we feel the enemy tempting us to finger-point, we can easily transform that urge into the powerful presence of God in our lives and words.

> "Yet I know that you are most holy; it's indisputable. You are God-Enthroned, surrounded with songs, living among the shouts of praise of your princely people" (Psalm 22.3 TPT).

**Three: Replace Finger-Pointing with Power.**

The power of God ignites in us when we obey Him. One thing is for sure, He doesn't like finger-pointing. In fact, the Bible says that Jesus came to save the world, not condemn it (John 3.17). Instead of laying blame, Jesus took the sins of the world on His back, dying to give us the ability to have a relationship with a Holy God. If Jesus could set aside finger-pointing, so can we. Once we do, we will literally have the resurrection power resting on us. The choice is easy. If we want the power of God in our lives, we must lay finger-pointing aside.

> "I want to know Christ and experience the mighty power that raised him from the dead. I want to suffer with him, sharing in his death, so that one way or another I will experience the resurrection from the dead!" (Philippians 3.10-11 NLT).

**Four: Stop Finger-Pointing towards Yourself.**

Did you know that criticizing yourself is just as bad as criticizing others? Some people wonder why, though they've learned to stop criticizing others, they still don't have the power of God in their lives. Might it be that they are still laying blame on their own heart daily? Nitpicking, finger-pointing and shaming oneself is not of God. The grace and forgiveness of Christ are rightfully ours by faith, and we must learn to extend it to ourselves.

When we feel the desire to withhold mercy from our own lives, we must instead replace our finger-pointing with prayer and praise. Yes, we can pray for ourselves too! Once we understand that we are dead to complaining, criticizing and finger-pointing, we will finally embrace the joy, hope and power that is rightfully our as co-heirs with Christ.

> "And since we are his children, we are his heirs. In fact, together with Christ we are heirs of God's glory.

But if we are to share his glory, we must also share his suffering" (Romans 8.17 NLT).

# DAY 35

## [4 WAYS WE GROW SPIRITUALLY]

God designed us. He gave us strengths that help us achieve our destiny in Him. He gave us weaknesses that help us achieve our intimacy with Him. Our weaknesses motivate us to rely on God (2 Corinthians 12.9). Our troubles remind us that we need Him (2 Corinthians 1.9).

God grows us spiritually by stretching our character and capacity. We are like earthen vessels that can be filled with His glory (2 Corinthians 4.7). The wider our borders, the more He can fill us and our lives with His presence. However, the devil will try to sabotage our borders by looking for weaknesses. Therefore, spiritual growth also includes taking spiritual inventory.

**Growing Spiritually Way 1: Stretch.**

God stretches us by allowing us to grow through difficulty. He places promises in our heart that we are unable to achieve without maturing in faith. As we chase these promises, our capacity expands, and we begin to grow spiritually.

> "Enlarge your house; build an addition. Spread out your home, and spare no expense!" (Isaiah 54.2 NLT).

**Growing Spiritually Way 2: Inspect.**

176

As God extends our capacity, we must then inspect. We can objectively look at both our strengths and weaknesses. We don't have to feel guilty or defensive. God is not trying to shame us. He wants to empower us in all areas.

> "Examine yourselves to see if your faith is genuine. Test yourselves. Surely you know that Jesus Christ is among you; if not, you have failed the test of genuine faith" (2 Corinthians 13.5 NLT).

**Growing Spiritually Way 3: Erect.**

Once we inspect, we can flag any areas of weakness. The devil loves to find ways to attack us and sabotage what God's doing in our lives (1 Peter 5.8 NLT). We have to see our weaknesses first before we can insulate them with Christ's power. Once we flag all the weak areas, we can erect Jesus as our defense in those areas.

> "Each time he said, 'My grace is all you need. My power works best in weakness.' So now I am glad to boast about my weaknesses, so that the power of Christ can work through me" (2 Corinthians 12.9 NLT).

**Growing Spiritually Way 4: Rest.**

Finally, we must rest in the Lord. God loves when we depend and lean on Him. He has an abundance of love, provision, healing, peace and rest to give us. No matter how much we grow spiritually, God always wants us to rely on Him.

"Then Jesus said, "Come to me, all of you who are weary and carry heavy burdens, and I will give you rest'" (Matthew 11.28 NLT).

Now we can be strong in Christ knowing that our strengths are submitted to Him and our weaknesses defended by Him.

# DAY 36

## [2 MYTHS AND 2 BREAKTHROUGHS ON STRETCHING]

"Enlarge the place of your tent, stretch your tent curtains wide, do not hold back; lengthen your cords, strengthen your stakes" (Isaiah 54.2 NIV).

If you were to compare your muscles to a rubber band, the more you would stretch them, the more worn out and prone to snapping they would become. It is a myth to think we can stretch and make our muscles longer. So what are we really doing when we "stretch"?

When we stretch, we are aiming to relax our muscles to alleviate muscles tension. Plus, we are showing our nervous system that the greater range of motion is safe.

**Myth 1: Stretch Against the Tension.**

Our muscles resist lengthening to their full size not because they are short. They resist because they are tense. Muscle tension, tight muscles, body stiffness and headaches are all common symptoms of stress. When we learn to relax, much of our muscle aches and pains would subside. Instead of fighting our contracted muscles by stretching against the tension, we can learn to relax our entire body, and the muscles would become more pliable and lengthen naturally.

**Myth 2: Stretching Should be Uncomfortable.**

There are nerves all over our body, and when we do movements that our muscles are not accustomed to, like touching our toes, our nerves send off warning signals to our nervous system. So our muscles resist the stretch because our body doesn't think it's safe. We don't normally move that far. If we were to make those movements several times a week, our nerves would grow accustomed to the stretch and stop firing off warning signals. Little by little we gain range of motion not because our muscles are longer, but because our nervous system begins to trust the new capacity.

**When God Spiritual Stretches You.**

**Breakthrough 1:**

When we trust God with our lives, we will learn to relax under His authority. Our mistrust of Him creates tension, causing emotional, spiritual, mental and physical aches and pains in our lives. How do we learn to trust God more? By learning more about Him. The best way to fully know and embrace God's love through Jesus Christ is to spend time praying and reading His Word. Once we know for ourselves how loving God truly is and how He has our best interests at heart, we will not only relax, but we will enjoy life.

> "No wonder my heart is glad, and I rejoice. My body rests in safety" (Psalm 16.9 NLT).

**Breakthrough 2:**

God wants to increase our capacity, so we can do more for His Kingdom. At first, when God puts us into a new circumstance, we may feel fear and anxiety. Our minds are signaling to us that we are in a new and uncomfortable situation. But if we continue in that same circumstance day after day, what was once scary to us will soon become our new normal. Our range of motion in life will increase little by little as we trust God and overcome our fear with faith. We will grow in our capacity, authority and influence and steadily become accustomed to greater acts of obedience.

> "Whoever can be trusted with very little can also be trusted with much..." (Luke 16.10 NIV)

.

# DAY 37

## [3 WAYS TO HEAR FROM GOD]

"...Listen for God's voice in everything you do, everywhere you go; he's the one who will keep you on track..." (Proverbs 3.6 MSG).

Moses led God's people out of slavery into the wilderness, so they could learn to hear God's voice. All of us are in some form of bondage – a way of believing and living that is not God's best. God must lead us into the wilderness – a transition that helps us hear Him – so we can step into our Promised Land (Exodus).

What happens in the wilderness is a three-step process that opens the way for God's Spirit (the Holy Spirit) to be unleashed in our lives, so we can hear from Him every day.

- First, we are thrown.
- Second, we are broken.
- Third, we can listen.

Water represents the Holy Spirit and there was a lack of it in the desert, which caused the people to cry out to God. They had to learn to lean on Him and listen to His voice in the wilderness. When we leave our bondage, we too lack the fullness of God's Spirit in our lives. So, God must throw us and break us, so we learn how to hear Him. Then, all He needs is to speak and our ears are open.

**First, Moses Threw a Tree into the Bitter Water to Make it Sweet.**

> "So Moses cried out to the Lord for help, and the Lord showed him a piece of wood. Moses threw it into the water, and this made the water good to drink..." (Exodus 15.25 NLT).

Many times, it feels like God throws us, so He can turn our bitterness into sweetness. We live our days so accustomed to personal bondage that God must literally throw us into new circumstances to get our attention. Loss of a job, bad medical report, a cheating spouse, a wayward child – all throw us into what feels like chaos, but God is ready to catch us in the pools of His grace. The Wood of the Cross turns our bitterness into something sweet.

**Second, Moses Struck the Rock, so Water Could Pour Forth.**

> "'I will stand before you on the rock at Mount Sinai. Strike the rock, and water will come gushing out. Then the people will be able to drink.' So Moses struck the rock as he was told, and water gushed out as the elders looked on" (Exodus 17.6 NLT).

Once we are thrown out of our comfort zones, God will strike us, breaking all our control and self-reliance. The breaking is a beautiful, yet painful process. The breaking allows us to become malleable to the shaping and pruning of God's Hands. It is also when we truly learn to rely on and hear from God.

**Third, Moses was Supposed to Speak to the Rock, but He Disobeyed.**

> "You and Aaron must take the staff and assemble the entire community. As the people watch, speak to the rock over there, and it will pour out its water. You will provide enough water from the rock to satisfy the whole community and their livestock" (Numbers 20.8 NLT).

Instead of speaking to the rock, Moses disobeyed and struck the rock twice. Because of his sin, he was not allowed to enter the Promised Land (Numbers 20.12). Why was God mad? Because striking was no longer needed. The people were ready to listen and hear God's commands. God will not strike our lives more than we can handle. Once our ears are directed to Him, we can hear His whisper clearly.

> "...And after the fire there was the sound of a gentle whisper" (1 Kings 19.12 NLT).

This is an awesome reminder to us today. Yes, God may have to throw our lives into our destiny. And He may have to break us to mold us. But eventually we will become sensitive to His voice. At His Word alone, our lives will be filled with His moving Spirit.

# DAY 38

# [6 SIMPLE FOOD CHOICES TO LOSE WEIGHT]

Instead of always struggling to lose weight, you can make these 6 simple choices every day and maintain your desired weight for life.

We always see those people who never seem to gain weight. We wonder what they are doing to keep the weight off. Do they have some sort of superpower that we don't? Is there a secret they are hiding from us? The answer is no. These people who maintain a healthy weight incorporate these 6 simple food choices into their diets. These choices will not only help you to lose weight, but they will help you to keep the weight off with simple healthy changes.

**1. Lose Weight by Replacing Carbs with Veggies.**

Bread consumption should be saved for a slice of wonderful, handmade bread that's worth the calories. Processed breads are not worth your time. Instead of having toast with your eggs, replace it with grilled veggies. Instead of having a bun on your sandwich, replace it with a lettuce wrap. Instead of having rice with chicken curry, replace it with steamed broccoli. And instead of having egg noodles with beef stroganoff, replace the pasta with roasted Brussels sprouts. Replace your breads and carbs with veggies and you will lose weight.

**2. Lose Weight by Replacing Sweets with Fruit.**

We all like desserts. But eating sweets every day will add on the weight. Instead of high sugar processed sweets, always have fruit ready to be washed and eaten. Apples are very sweet and filling. Berries are chock-full of vitamins. Oranges are awesome when you feel under the weather. And grapes are great to snack on while watching a movie. Replace your sweets with fruit and you will drop the weight.

**3. Lose weight by Replacing Sodas with Water.**

People today are chronically dehydrated. Our bodies are crying out for water, but we confuse the signal for thirst with hunger. We would lose weight if we simply drank the recommended 8 glasses of water a day instead of sodas and other high sugar drinks. Replacing sodas with water (or unsweet flavored water or tea) will help you lose weight and stay healthy.

**4. Lose Weight by Replacing Junk Food with Healthy Snacks.**

It is hard to concentrate when we are hungry. We may be tempted to grab a processed snack on the go. Instead, we can begin to find healthy snacks to replace those unhealthy, processed snacks. You can keep a bag of lightly salted almonds handy. Or you can have cubed or string cheese waiting in the refrigerator. Carrots and hummus is a filling snack that will quickly alleviate hunger pains. Replace junk food with healthy snacks and the weight will come off.

**5. Lose Weight by Replacing Sauces/Dressing on Your Food to Sauces/Dressing on the Side.**

Sometimes a salad will come to your table overflowing with dressing. We become used to tasting only ranch, honey mustard or blue cheese. But the veggies in the salad are what taste so great! Ask for the salad dressing on the side. Same goes with sauces. Sauces allow a plain piece of meat to have some flavor, but it doesn't need to run down the meat. Ask for sauces on the side too, so you can control how much you put on. A little goes a long way, and you will lose weight by keeping sauces and dressings at healthy portion sizes.

**6. Lose Weight by Replacing Pastries with Dark Chocolate.**

When your body is craving a pastry, it is best to skip the donuts, pies and cakes. Just have dark chocolate without the other carbs and fats that desserts usually contain. Keep dark chocolate in the fridge when your cravings get the better of you. Dark chocolate also has antioxidants and other health benefits. Eating it in moderation will help you avoid calorie-dense desserts, so you can lose weight while keeping your sweet tooth satisfied.

# Day 39

# [5 WAYS JESUS CAN CHANGE YOUR EMOTIONS]

**How Jesus Changed My Emotions.**

I remember one night in 2012, God was leading me to do something that was crazy, frowned upon and definitely not on my list of to-dos. He told me to self-publish my debut novel, Eve of Awakening. I had finished writing the book in December of 2005 and for over seven years I did everything God asked me to do from letting it sit for years while I raised my three babies, to mailing out queries, to hiring an editor, to finding an agent, to sending it to book competitions, to attending writers conferences and to rewriting and editing the book several times. All this work and at the end of the day, He said to self-publish. Absolutely not!

I sat on the floor in my kitchen and cried out to God. He wouldn't lead me down this path, would He? Was I not good enough for a traditional publisher? The answer to obey was not in my heart, and if He wanted to change my mind, He would have to do it supernaturally. And so He did.

Right there on the kitchen floor, the thickest peace poured over me and across my spirit. The kitchen was filled with it. I still didn't agree with His decision, but I couldn't deny the divine peace that blanketed me. Jesus literally transformed my emotional state. So I obeyed.

188

Since that night I chose to obey, I have published over 30 books and over 200 writers. I still don't understand the fullness of God's plan in my life, but I trust that God will give me an emotional loophole when I need it.

**How Can Jesus Change Your Emotions?**

We can't always control how we feel; however, as Christ-followers we have a divine loophole. Jesus overrides all our emotions if we surrender to His power and authority.

In the Bible, Jesus gives us His two greatest commands: to love God and to love others (Mark 12.30-31). But if we can't control how we feel, there is no way we will be able to obey, right? Is God setting us up for failure, commanding us to do the impossible?

What we find is Jesus set the highest standard, knowing we would fall short and that He would have to accomplish it on our behalf.

> "Do not think that I have come to abolish the Law or the Prophets; I have not come to abolish them but to fulfill them. For truly, I say to you, until heaven and earth pass away, not an iota, not a dot, will pass from the Law until all is accomplished" (Matthew 5.17-18 ESV).

Not only can we love when we don't feel like it, but we can also have peace instead of frustration; strength instead of timidity; joy instead of sorrow and discipline instead of chaos. This doesn't mean we won't experience the full spectrum of emotions, but if God gives us a command that we don't "feel" like obeying, He will give us an emotional loophole, if we let Him. When God changes our feelings, it will be possible to obey.

**Jesus Can Transform Your Emotions.**

If God is asking you to do something difficult, scary or countercultural, ask Him to "cheat" on your behalf by giving you His feelings on the matter. He sees what we can't see and knows what we don't know. God is the ultimate winner in the end, and we can obey His commands knowing that we have the victory with Him.

> "But thanks be to God! He gives us the victory through our Lord Jesus Christ" (1 Corinthians 15.57 NIV).

Whatever you are facing, ask God to overhaul your emotions, so you can obey His command. You might not be able to change how you feel, but Jesus can.

**ONE: Claim the Resurrected Emotions of Jesus.**

Are you having trouble with negative emotions? When we submit our emotions to God, they must obey Him. Everything submitted to God obeys. And when they obey, He can move powerfully through them! God loves transforming our emotions into powerful feelings that are pleasing to Him.

> "The disciples were absolutely terrified. 'Who is this man?' they asked each other. 'Even the wind and waves obey him!'" (Mark 4.41 NLT).

**TWO: The Emotion of Love instead of Hate.**

Are you struggling with anger? Even if that person has hurt you wrongfully, the emotion of hate will be a rot in your soul. God is the Ultimate Judge. Give Him your anger. Let Him deal with that person or situation, so you can walk in the freedom of love.

> "And hope does not put us to shame, because God's love has been poured out into our hearts through the Holy Spirit, who has been given to us" (Romans 5.5 NIV).

**THREE: The Emotion of Peace instead of Chaos.**

Is there chaos all around you? You can have peace in the eye of the storm. Jesus promises us His peace. Stay close to Him and the storms of life won't knock you down.

> "Peace I leave with you; my peace I give you. I do not give to you as the world gives. Do not let your hearts be troubled and do not be afraid" (John 14.27 NIV).

**FOUR: The Emotion of Strength instead of Weakness.**

Do you feel weak? God's strength is strong in your weakness if you submit it to Him. Everyone has weaknesses. They are nothing to be ashamed of. You simply need to surrender them to God and watch His power rise up in you.

> "That's why I take pleasure in my weaknesses, and in the insults, hardships, persecutions, and troubles that I suffer for Christ. For when I am weak, then I am strong" (2 Corinthians 12.10 NLT).

**FIVE: The Emotion of Joy instead of Sorrow.**

Do you have sorrow? We live in a fallen world. Life is not perfect, and the heartaches should push us to God. Give Him your grief and allow Him to fill you with His joy.

> "May the God of hope fill you with all joy and peace as you trust in him, so that you may overflow with hope by the power of the Holy Spirit" (Romans 15.13 NIV).

**SIX: The Emotion of Motivation instead of Laziness.**

Are you unmotivated? Sometimes the greatest path God is calling us to is the hardest route to walk. It can be daunting trying to get motivated when the journey seems difficult and long. But God will be with us every step of the way. We just need His supernatural motivation by believing He has great plans for us.

> "For I know the plans I have for you,' declares the Lord, 'plans to prosper you and not to harm you, plans to give you hope and a future" (Jeremiah 29.11 NIV).

# Day 40

# [6 LETTERS: THE ABCS OF ACHIEVING PEACE]

**Letter A: Your Attitude.**

> "Finally, brothers and sisters, whatever is true, whatever is noble, whatever is right, whatever is pure, whatever is lovely, whatever is admirable—if anything is excellent or praiseworthy—think about such things" (Philippians 4.8 NIV).

As the saying goes, attitude is everything. It is the one thing in life that we can control. We can wake up on the right side of the bed or the wrong side according to our attitude. We can make it a daily routine to wake up and instantly check our thoughts. We have been saved from the depths of hell through the Finished Work of Jesus Christ on the Cross. Nothing is worse than eternity separated from God. We have so much to be grateful for. We must choose to walk in a positive attitude of peace from the start of every day.

**Letter B: Your Biology.**

> "This day the Lord will deliver you into my hands, and I'll strike you down and cut off your head. This very day I will give the carcasses of the Philistine army to the birds and the wild animals, and the whole world will know that there is a God in Israel" (1 Samuel 17.46 NIV).

When King David was young, he chose to fight Goliath. Although King David said that God would fight for him, he still needed a two-part offensive system to bring Goliath down. First, he needed a sling. Second, he needed a sword (the Bible). Some people have difficulty attaining peace due to biological and medical issues. In order to overcome, they need God's strength and a two-part offensive system of medical help and God's Word. With God and medicine, they can achieve peace until they are strong enough to cut off the giant's head themselves.

**Letter C: Your Circumstances.**

> "Dear brothers and sisters, when troubles of any kind come your way, consider it an opportunity for great joy. For you know that when your faith is tested, your endurance has a chance to grow. So let it grow, for when your endurance is fully developed, you will be perfect and complete, needing nothing" (James 1.2-4 NLT).

God uses our circumstances to mold us into the image of Jesus. Just like we go into a gym to add resistance against our muscles to grow them, God will allow resistance in our lives to grow us. We will not mature spiritually without circumstances that force us to grow. We can have peace in our circumstances because we know that nothing surprises God. He has allowed the circumstance for a reason. We maintain peace in the eye of the storm of our situation because God is there with us. God is mighty to calm even the wind and the waves of our minds, so we can have peace (Mark 4.39)

**Letter D: Your Design.**

"Three different times I begged the Lord to take it away. Each time he said, 'My grace is all you need. My power works best in weakness.' So now I am glad to boast about my weaknesses, so that the power of Christ can work through me. That's why I take pleasure in my weaknesses, and in the insults, hardships, persecutions, and troubles that I suffer for Christ. For when I am weak, then I am strong" (2 Corinthians 12.8-10 NLT).

Every person is different. We all have strengths, and we all have weaknesses. Many times, our greatest strengths are stemmed to our greatest weaknesses. God designed us uniquely to fulfill a special purpose. Both our strengths and weaknesses will propel us to our destiny if they are submitted to God. Our weaknesses do not have to rob us of our peace. We will never be perfect, but we can have a relationship with the One Who is. God's power is made perfect in our weakness. They keep us humble and reliant on God. We can have peace knowing that He designed us wonderfully (Psalm 139.14).

**Letter E: Your Emotions.**

"The heart is deceitful above all things and beyond cure. Who can understand it?" (Jeremiah 17.9 NIV).

We are emotional beings. Just like anything, our emotions can be used for good or evil whether or not they are submitted to God. The truth is that sometimes our feelings can't be trusted. If what we feel contradicts what we know in God's Word to be true, it can cause disturbances in our lives. We must choose to exchange our worries, anxiety, fears, and insecurities for God's peace. His peace is always there ready to be received. If our emotions get in the way of that peace, we may need to close the door on them for a while.

**Letter F: Your Family.**

> "And we know that in all things God works for the good of those who love him, who have been called according to his purpose" (Romans 8.28 NIV).

Our family and childhood do much to shape who we are. We can inherit family strengths and strongholds. Family dynamics (birth order, divorce, parental figures) and childhood experiences all influence us and create possible doors of disturbance in our lives. God gave us our family and upbringing for a reason. He can use all things for His good. We can have peace with our family by offering forgiveness, mercy, and grace. We can work closely with the Holy Spirit, so He can reshape any soul patterns we inherited that are not God's best.

I pray that these 40 days have blessed you. My hope for you is that you can reframe your perceptions with God's Truth, so your mind, heart and choices will follow Him into His best for your life. If you enjoyed this book, I would be grateful for a review on Amazon. You can find my other non-fiction and fiction books there or on my blog, www.alisahopewagner.com

*- alisa*

197

Made in the USA
Monee, IL
29 July 2022

10315432R00108